SOCIAL PSYCHOLOGY AND
INDIVIDUAL VALUES

978 0090 426 324

Politics

Editor

PROFESSOR W. A. ROBSON

Professor Emeritus of Public Administration in the University of London

SOCIAL PSYCHOLOGY
AND INDIVIDUAL VALUES

D. W. Harding

Professor of Psychology in the University of London

HUTCHINSON UNIVERSITY LIBRARY
LONDON

HUTCHINSON & CO (*Publishers*) LTD

178–202 Great Portland Street, London W1

London Melbourne Sydney
Auckland Bombay Toronto
Johannesburg New York

★

First published June 1953
Second impression (revised edition) July 1963
Third impression January 1966

This book has been set in Bembo, printed in Great Britain
on Smooth Wove paper by Anchor Press, and
bound by Wm. Brendon, both of Tiptree, Essex

CONTENTS

TO
MAY SMITH

PREFACE

In my treatment of social psychology in this book I have hoped to be of use to readers whose interest is chiefly in the implications of the subject for the broader concerns of social life and culture. They will not want an elementary account in psychological terms of politics, education, industrial relations, family life, religion and the arts: but they may wish to know which of the problems of his own subject a social psychologist regards as relevant to these matters of general importance and how his discipline attempts to handle them. In this book the emphasis falls upon the definition of problems and the broad conclusions towards which psychological inquiry and observation seem to be leading; less attention is given to the methods elaborated in seeking answers to the detailed questions (especially of applied psychology) into which many of the topics proliferate. Other psychologists would emphasise other problems and other ways of approaching them, and I hope that enough references are included to carry readers to different treatments of the subject, from which they can judge which developments hold promise. Social psychology has not yet acquired any valid claim to unintelligibility, and it is still malleable enough to benefit from the attention and the questions of educated men and women.

Bedford College
University of London
October, 1952

                              D. W. HARDING

I

SOCIAL DESIRE IN HUMAN BEINGS

Biologists are inclined to view all animals as social and to treat the 'solitary animal' as a myth (cf. Allee, 1939). Admittedly every animal must come to some accommodation with others of its species and the higher animals need at least sexual contact with a mate and parental care in early life. Biologists can hold these questions at arm's length, and their arm is as long as evolutionary time. Psychologists must take a nearer view and attend more closely to the differences in social behaviour between one species and another. At that range the outstanding fact is the vast diversity among species in the forms of their sociability. Between the cat tribe and the wolf tribe, the grisly bear and the bison, the hare and the rabbit, the robin and the rook, differences in sociability are strikingly evident. The full extent of the differences, both in degree and in kind, among the animal species is far from having been thoroughly studied. The familiar rough distinction between the gregarious and the non-gregarious (with the possibility of alternation between the two in the same species at different seasons) is useful as far as it goes but we have to be careful not to suppose that all sociability is gregarious. The social responsiveness of the domestic cat, for instance, can be highly developed but it remains strictly selective and is not accompanied by gregarious tendencies in the adults of the species.

The status of sociability in human beings is a matter of disagreement among psychologists. Two broad divisions of opinion are found:

(a) that it is in the nature of man to value the friendly companion-ship of others, as it is in his nature to value food and sleep: and,

(b) that there is no such innate basis of social behaviour and that our valuation of others is *derived* from some other features of our make-up.

Of this second division of opinion, the simplest variant is the view that sociability is a habit acquired because of its usefulness in contributing to the satisfaction of the individual's other needs. It was put forward by the behaviourists (e.g. F. H. Allport, 1924) and has appealed to many American sociologists. Kimball Young (1946) asserts that social behaviour is built up on the foundation of the infant's need for sustenance, warmth and physical safety, the satisfaction of these needs always being associated with the presence and assistance of other people, whose approval therefore comes to have a value which the later institutions of childhood and adult life serve to reinforce.

Freud, too, falls into this broad division of opinion. His views on the nature of social impulse were various and seem not to have been fully unified into a theory. They included the notion that men banded together because they had learned the advantages of co-operation for meeting their individual demands for food, shelter and protection, this notion being really an intellectualised way of putting the view that social habits develop in infancy because all our physical satisfactions are associated with the presence of human well-wishers. But the main Freudian contribution is the more general theory that people are bound together by goal-inhibited libidinal impulses; or, roughly, that liking and affection of all kinds are the outcome of unconscious sexual desire (whether hetero-sexual or homosexual) which have been 'goal-inhibited' in the sense of having been prevented from becoming conscious as recognisable sexual desire. The difficulty is to see why sexual desire should be goal-inhibited, except as a *result* of social organisation; what arises as a result of social life can scarcely be its cause as well. No effective escape from this circular argument is provided by Freud's further suggestion that human society grew out of a primal horde in which a patriarch had a sexual monopoly of the women until his sons revolted and killed him, thereafter being bound together by common remorse and a guilt-ridden renunciation of the incestuous impulses they had shared. The origin both of the horde and of the remorse and guilt has still to be explained.

More significant than the detailed argument, however, is the conviction, implicit in all that Freud says on the subject, that social life, with its restrictions on individual impulse, must in some way be thrust on the individual or offered him as a substitute for something else. A spontaneous liking for one's fellows and their companionship, arising in its own right and not derived from sexual desire, apparently never appeared to him as a possibility worth considering.

These peculiarities of the Freudian position were pointed out effectively by Suttie (1935), whose whole treatment of social life implied the belief that a potentiality for valuing affection and companionship is part of our native endowment. Yet Suttie hesitated to commit himself clearly to this view; his account seems at times to derive social desire from the affection felt for the mother in infancy, with a gradual extension of liking to the people whom she values. Admittedly, the first expression of a tendency to value others will be affectionate response to the mother, but we have to avoid the fallacy (not uncommon among psycho-analytic writers) of supposing that the first manifestation of a tendency is its origin. It would be at least misleading to say that the grown cat's mousing was 'derived' from the kitten's aptness to chase and pounce on blown leaves and bits of paper that move; it is equally misleading to say with Susan Isaacs (1933, p. 225) that the desire for property arises from the infant's wish to possess the breast securely; or to say that social desire is 'derived from' the affection felt by the infant for the mother. We are fully entitled to maintain that social desire arises directly from an innate disposition, while still recognising that it will show itself first in affectionate response to the mother and will find its later expressions in an extension of social responsiveness under her influence.

Suttie was needlessly uneasy at postulating an inborn capacity for affectionate response, as distinct from the Freudian sexuality. He created a difficulty by assuming that inborn capacities or dispositions must be accompanied by specially differentiated physical structures, such as those for eating and copulating; in the end, he allayed his doubts by suggesting that the organs of speech were the differentiated structures that served social needs, allowing us to express vocally our interest in one another. But this was unnecessary. Other inborn capacities, besides that for sociability, make use of physical equipment that serves more than one purpose. Anger and combat, for example, call on much the same muscular and glandular mechanisms as fear and flight, merely activating them in a different total pattern. Impulses to explore and construct similarly lack any structural equipment for their exclusive use. There would be nothing exceptional in the fact that a readiness to value others should be part of our native constitution and yet have no peculiar organ of expression, but should instead make use in caresses of the same muscles as we use for attack, and in welcoming gurgles and endearments the same vocal apparatus that serves to express terror or pain.

Theories of an indirect derivation of social desire, by acquired habit or through unconscious transformations, are open to the objections of being unnecessarily elaborate and also of making it more difficult to explain observed differences in the form of social life peculiar to the various species. The Freudian theory of trans-formed sexuality, for instance, can give no clue to the reason for differences between gregarious and non-gregarious animals all of which have sexual needs. The view that social responsiveness grows out of early response to parental care seems difficult to harmonise with the fact that both gregarious and less widely sociable animals go through an early period of maternal care; on this view, indeed, one would have reversed the facts and imagined that the cat tribe, born in a litter and engaging in play together during early life, would grow up to be gregarious; and that cattle, generally coming one at a birth, would not. This evidence from animal behaviour strongly suggests that differences in the form taken by the social impulse are part of the native endowment of the species and define themselves in mature behaviour regardless of, and perhaps in defiance of, some experiences of early life.

Varieties of sociability that arise from the native constitution of the different species are, of course, interlocked with other native differences, such as the characteristic modes of food-seeking and defence. For instance, the seeking of safety in prompt and rapid flight rather than concealment is to some extent favoured by life in a herd or flock with sentinel eyes in all directions; and the hunting of prey by stealthy approach or lurking, instead of running it down by scent and speed, is likely to be most effective in association with a solitary way of life. It seems probable that a native readiness for some particular kind and degree of sociability is often a necessary condition of the full effectiveness of other tendencies and equipment with which a species is endowed. This is certainly suggested by the dispersal of the young of certain 'solitary' animals when they reach early maturity, a dispersal which involves the disruption of the earlier habit of dependent sociability.

If other animal species have a natural tendency towards some form of sociability or solitariness it seems reasonable to suppose that man has also, and his sociability, displayed wherever he is found and usually involving some degree of gregariousness, may plausibly be regarded as 'natural' to him. Undoubtedly it is modified and diversified by cultural acquisitions, but these seem to be superimposed on an inborn capacity to welcome the society of others. To suppose otherwise, with those psychologists who argue that social desire must be derived from or transformed from some other human need, involves the much less economical belief that man as an animal species is non-gregarious, but has had society by some means thrust upon it, and thrust upon it the whole world over.

We seem justified in assuming that the observed sociability of man is based, with whatever accretions from cultural accident, on a natural disposition of the species. What more accurate account of this 'natural disposition' can be given?

Early this century the dynamic psychologists of the time described it as a herd instinct or gregarious instinct. Trotter's classic work, *The Instincts of the Herd in Peace and War* (1916), was based on this conception, which had earlier been put forward by McDougall (1908) and was retained by him (1932) under the changed name of the 'gregarious propensity', the propensity to remain in the company of our fellows and to seek to rejoin them if we become isolated. The conception of instinct in psychology has caused great difficulties, and although there has recently been a renewed recognition of McDougall's grasp of the crucial problem (cf. W. S. Hunter, 1947), few people would want to return to anything like the old reliance on instincts as explanations of behaviour. We would not now take seriously the suggestion made by McDougall in the early book (1908) that increasing urbanisation occurred because the traditions and economic needs that kept people widely scattered over the country were weakening and so giving fuller scope to the instinctive tendency to flock together. As several writers have pointed out, such an idea goes too far, since the impulse to join large herds is one from which many human beings are free, and it fails to go far enough, since merely being together seems to be less important to us than doing things together. Ginsberg (1932) prefers the more general formulation of a 'root interest' of sociality which leads to various specialised responses to others, with a craving for response from them.

In any case, it would not be enough to label sociability an 'instinct' and leave it at that, for the 'instincts' included in McDougall's list were not by any means all the same kind of psycho-physical pattern of behaviour. As Drever (1917) pointed out, some (such as those for food, sleep and sexual activity) are appetitive, arising directly as primary impulses of the animal, whereas others are reactive, arising only contingently according as the primary needs are satisfied or not; thus pugnacity is called into play not as a primary impulse but as an adjunct to the satisfaction of another desire which is threatened with obstruction. One must make the further distinction between those 'instincts' which are cyclic appetites and others which are continually developing interests: the appetite for food, for example, takes the form of a growing desire, a satisfying activity, latency of the appetite, and then renewal of the desire in more or less its original form; but the urges to explore and construct have little cyclic character, and although they present us with particular goals for the time being the achievement of one goal brings into view another, more advanced, and when the urge is renewed we are not simply back at the original desire. Different again from the cyclic appetites with their fairly periodic demands are the needs, such as the need for air or for a certain range of warmth, which we become aware of mainly when satisfaction is denied.

This last characteristic appears in social desire, at least in many of its manifestations. It would be a mistake of emphasis to speak with Ginsberg of 'response and craving for response' if this were taken to imply that our social needs are chiefly satisfied in active spells of mutual response during which the other person is given our focal attention. That occurs no doubt in certain phases and aspects of social development; between mother and infant, for example, and in some intense friendship and love, the mutual responsiveness is the central part of the experience. But most of our social satisfaction is totally different, and it is not just a low intensity of the same reciprocal interest. Suttie (1935) made the valuable point that in healthy psychological development the mutual absorption of infant and mother is gradually replaced by an outward turning of attention which gives them the satisfaction of sharing an interest in something outside them both. For the child, this phase initiates the main form of social satisfaction, that of knowing that our interests are shared and our sentiments and attitudes given sympathy; it is the satisfaction of knowing that the scale of values expressed in what we do is sanctioned and supported by other people. They may make their sanction felt by sharing our activity; on the other hand, they may be nowhere near us and we gain social sanction by knowing that our activities have a niche in the structure of our social group. Lonely explorers, adventurers in aircraft or on rafts or into the higher mathematics can feel that whether or not their achievements are fully understood the value of their activity is recognised by the group to which they belong.

Whether we speak of a social instinct, or a disposition, or a root interest, we shall mislead ourselves if we imply that active response to one another is the chief feature of people's social life. What we want most of the time is an awareness of friendly companionship in *other* activities, not specifically social ones. Nor should we speak with Kimball Young (1946) of the 'recurrent' need for security; the need for the security given by social sanction is permanent, pervading all our activities, like the need for a certain range of physical warmth. It seems that human beings value the sense of being socially sanctioned in as wide a range of their activities as possible, whether their range is small and simple or extensive and complex.

It may be that the 'gregarious instinct' of lower animals is much the same thing at a simpler level: the desire not merely to be in a herd but to have similarly occupied companions about you while you graze or ruminate or seek out the shade. The importance of this sanctioning companionship in facilitating other activities is suggested by the experimental work of Katz (1937) in showing that hens would eat more grain if they were in company with others than if they were alone; and by the observation of Fraser Darling (1938) that the mating activities of some birds will go forward with sufficient vigour for the effective reproduction of the species only if they occur amidst the excitement of a large colony similarly engaged.

The core of an adequate account of social impulse is the recognition that a social animal values its companions for some quality other than their usefulness as animate objects in the environment. Failure to recognise this mars the interpretation given by Miller and Dollard (1945) of their ingenious experiments in which rats were taught to accept the 'leadership' of other rats that had already learned their way about an elevated maze. Demonstrating that a rat would learn to follow the lead of another rat if he regularly led it to food, these authors suggested that even complex instances of dependence, such as a human being's dependence on a political leader, illustrate the same process. But the experiment gave no evidence whatever that the leader rat was more than an environmental cue to the other, an animate object that served as a signal and was psychologically equivalent to any other cue that might have been used, such as a black or a white card. If this were 'social' psychology we should have no need of the adjective; it would mean that people have no more significance than any other usable bit of the environment. If the leader rat was, in fact, *merely* instrumental in the satisfaction of the other rat's desire for food then he had ecological but not social significance.

The kind of behaviour towards other people that would naturally ensue from failing to experience them as something more than animate objects can sometimes be seen on the part of the so-called psychopathic personality when it occurs in conjunction with good intelligence. Then the show of considerateness (with occasional astonishing lapses), the suave friendliness of manner, the insincerity and the total self-centredness give a hint of the quality of group life that would result if our social behaviour consisted of acquired habits and skills serving exclusively non-social needs. We need not sentimentally under-estimate the extent of egocentricity and insincerity all around and within us, or the extent to which we reduce other people to the status of tools for our purposes; but, in addition to all this, as a thread running through it and occasionally appearing (in some people and in some situations often appearing), there is in most human beings a spontaneous liking for the friendly companionship of other living beings.

Psychologically one has to be as clear as possible as to what is meant, and still more what is not meant, by suggesting that this liking for others is an inborn disposition. To begin with, whether we call it an instinct or an innate drive or an inherited pattern of response, it is not a something which is any more mysterious than the rest of living activity. Given time, lots of time, physiology will presumably be able to show upon what chemical and electrical processes and patterns it depends. Already something is known of the hormonal influences that activate (which, of course, is not the same as producing) the alternate patterns of behaviour in some species of birds that flock together amicably at one season of the year and at other times pugnaciously defend individual territories (cf. Fraser Darling, 1938). But as Beach (1948) has adequately shown, the explanatory reach of endocrinology into complex behaviour is still very limited. The psychologist will for long have to state as clearly as he can the observable facts of behaviour and experience, and leave it to future work, in neurology and biochemistry as well as in psychology, to illuminate the more intimate physical processes associated with their occurrence. If the dynamic processes culminating in certain forms of behaviour are described as 'instincts' or 'innate dispositions' this must not imply that they are mysterious entities that activate the organism and can be distinguished from the living functions and structures of which it consists.

Nor does an innate disposition to social responsiveness mean that some social craving will appear regardless of environmental influences. We have the instance of the 'wild boy' of Aveyron (Itard, trans. Humphrey, 1932) to witness that a child who lived without human care up to the age of about ten years was by then apparently incapable of ordinary social response in spite of five years' assiduous training. In a sufficiently unusual environmental setting, the natural dispositions of a species may fail to appear or may be greatly modified in expression. Thorpe (1963) shows how little of a bird's characteristic song develops if it never hears adults of the species sing; kittens reared together with young rats will not treat these or other rats as prey (Kuo, 1930); and birds unable to find the ordinary materials for their nests will make considerable changes in the usual structure in order to employ what materials are available. And yet birds have a natural disposition to sing and build nests in ways characteristic of their species, and cats as a species are natural predators on rats. To say that a liking for friendly companionship is part of human nature means that this liking will occur if it is given only that minimum environmental invitation found in the simplest conditions in which man can live as a viable species.

Even then one has to add two provisos. One is that individuals and ethnic groups may perhaps differ in their inborn capacity for social responsiveness and their need of it. We know nothing about this beyond the bare possibility. The second proviso is that accidents of cultural history may institutionalise barriers to the development of social response. In assessing the psychological significance of Dobuan culture, for instance, one would need more information than Fortune (1932) reported on the extent to which the Dobu people's sentiments of mutual hostility and distrust may have been induced in young children against some natural resistance. We have in the case of the Balinese an account (Bateson and Mead, 1942) of deliberate techniques of severe teasing by which any show of affectionate responsiveness and any betrayal of dependence on the liking of another person are drilled out of children; the resultant schizoid detachment in the adults is therefore demonstrably a cultural distortion of more natural impulses. It should, of course, be noted that even the people of Dobu are highly socialised and the efforts they make to get the better of one another are themselves an inverted expression of the importance they attach to each other's forced respect.

Societies like the Dobuan, in fact, only present in sharper form the difficulty, suggested by any human society, of believing that it is fundamentally a liking for each other that brings people together when in reality they spend a great part of their time bickering, robbing each other and making enemies. This feature of human society must be given attention later. For the moment, it is enough to recapitulate the general theme that animal species differ in their degree and form of sociability; and that the human species appears to be highly responsive socially. Although men engage in mutual hostilities it seems likely that, as part of their nature as an animal species, they tend readily to value the friendly companionship of others; what they value is the knowledge that their activities are going on in a congenial social context which gives them a sense of being sanctioned by those whom they value and whose activities they reciprocally sanction.

2

PUGNACITY IN SOCIAL LIFE[1]

The quantity and intensity of the antagonism generated in human beings against each other might seem to conflict with the belief in a natural tendency for men to value the friendly companionship of their kind. It has to be recognised that our desire for good relations with others is only one of many desires, and that beings as complex as men and living in so complex an environment will inevitably find many of their aims conflicting. The person whose companionship we value at one time is the same person who, at another time, deprives us of goods in short supply or tries to shape our lives to a pattern we detest. But, although hostility between individuals of a gregarious species is perfectly familiar, there is no doubt that pugnacity and antagonism amongst human beings, especially their expression in war, create not only terrifying practical prospects but moral and psychological problems as well.

Under the general heading of pugnacity we have to include both social and non-social behaviour. Struggling against a policeman who wants to arrest you, hacking at the tentacles of an octopus that seizes you, and cutting your way clear of brambles or wait-a-bit thorn in which you are entangled all seem to be examples of the same broad pattern of behaviour. Combative behaviour can be directed against inanimate objects and natural forces, against animals to whom we feel no social tie, against strangers of our own species

[1] This chapter is based, with the permission of the Editor, on a paper contributed to the *British Journal of Medical Psychology*, XXII, 1949, 161–5.

and against the fellow-members of our social group (apart from being sometimes directed against ourselves). At one end of that scale we can be pugnacious with an easy mind; but, when we reach the point of attacking other human beings, especially if they have some degree of companionship with us, then we find our combative behaviour more and more entangled with a sense of guilt or uneasiness or regret. We may feel righteously exhilarated by a successful attack with an axe against a tree that obstructs cultivation, but the after-effects are usually different if we raise the same axe against a member of our own species.

Obviously the sense of guilt is less the more certain we feel that our pugnacity is justified; hence international jockeying for moral position before embarking on war. Whether we can persuade ourselves, as nations or individual people, that our belligerent action is defensive will be crucial for our comfort of mind. Even when we do, defensive fighting may still leave behind a load of guilt-feelings when once the aggressor is sufficiently damaged to be no longer a menace, as we have seen in the English attitude to Germany after each of two wars. This kind of reaction (in personal as well as international affairs) inclines some psycho-analysts to the view that all 'aggression', provoked or not, induces a sense of guilt.

Psycho-analytic and some recent psychological writings have, in fact, added confusion to the question of pugnacity through using the word 'aggression', tinged as it is with the notion of unprovoked attack, to include an enormous range of behaviour and feeling, including the sentiment of hatred, any expression of anger, combat, pugnacity, malice, cruelty, brutality, destructiveness, assertiveness, vigorous efforts to overcome obstacles, and more besides. No doubt all these have something in common, but the tendency here, as elsewhere in psychology, has been towards impoverishing a rich and psychologically subtle language in return for a not very illuminating generalisation. In particular, nothing is gained by ignoring the fact that defensive combat and what genuinely strikes people as a morally justifiable use of force are real possibilities. Yet in this use of the term aggression, the analysts and psychologists have been responsive to a current of feeling among the educated people of their cultures, one which has emphasised the regrettable aspect of any use of force against others and encouraged suspicion about the arguments that justify it.

It is true that there are degrees of responsibility for outbreaks of hostility, whether wars or more domestic and personal quarrels. Yet measuring the degree of blame, going back over the ever-receding path of provocation and counter-provocation that led to the outbreak, involves a laborious and intricate post-mortem that never fully satisfies either side. With increasing maturity, of individual or group, there comes to be less interest in apportioning blame and justifying either partner in the mutual pugnacity, and much more concern to avoid in future the relation of hostility. Regret at the breach comes in time to outweigh the satisfaction of demonstrating one's guiltlessness.

This line of thought, or this development of social sentiment, finds support in some technical views in psychology, of which H. H. Anderson (1939) has given the barest and most exact statement. His work leads away from ethical debate about the justice or defensibility of this or that piece of combative behaviour and turns attention instead to the psychological possibility of a totally different kind of social action when the scene is set for a clash.

He sees the use of force as one means of domination, this term implying the imposition of our own aims on people who have different aims, whether we do so by force, guile, propaganda or appeals to affection. 'Persuasion' may or may not be dominative; it depends whether we meet objections and counter-persuasions with a genuinely open mind or whether we are rigidly committed to the end that we propose, however tactfully, to compass. Domination and submission, and attempted domination and resistance, express a deeply entrenched mode of handling differences of aim between human beings. 'Compromise' belongs to the same mode of social relation in so far as it consists in submission at some points in return for being allowed our own way at others. In contrast to this dominative way of dealing with differences of aim, Anderson draws attention to another, which he calls 'integrative'.

M. P. Follett had already used the term with broadly the same significance though rather more loosely. She thought of it largely as a process in which the two sides to a conflict reformulated their desires in such a way as to make them mutually compatible.

'This conception of the revaluation of desire it is necessary to keep in the foreground of our thinking in dealing with conflict, for neither side ever "gives in" really, it is hopeless to expect it, but there often comes a moment when there is a simultaneous revaluation of interests on both sides and unity precipitates itself' (Metcalf and Urwick, 1941).

In integrative behaviour the realisation that the other person or the other group sees things differently or is pursuing a different aim is welcomed by both parties as an opportunity from which may emerge, with further interchange, a new aim or outlook more satisfying to each side than the one it started with. This implies co-operation of a special kind: not the kind found when several people join together to carry out intentions formulated by one of them, or held independently by them all, but the kind that involves genuinely mutual influence in the arrival at the aim itself as well as the methods of carrying it out. It can be seen at times among the best members of the best committees, though domination (with submission or resistance) and the bargaining of compromise are more usual in committee work. It seldom occurs otherwise than sporadically and transiently, and people differ vastly in their readiness to attempt it and in their command of the techniques of social exchange that make it possible. Anderson has put into the discipline of quantitative assessment his observations of these differences as they occur between children and in the handling of children by teachers. The great value of his work has been to draw attention adequately, as a matter of technical psychology, to the fact that 'integrative behaviour' provides a mode of social relation qualitatively distinct from the dominative-submissive mode in which the greater part of social intercourse—including family life, discipline, trade, politics and war—is at present set.

Living in a dominative society makes it difficult for us to grasp the possible development of other methods of dealing with conflicts of aim, whether between individuals or between groups. The emphasis has for so long been on some form of domination, in restrictive discipline, ridicule, salesmanship, guile, propaganda, threatened withdrawal of affection, economic pressure, or open force, that for a very long time to come domination in the broad sense will be not only the last resort but the usual means of settling social differences and bringing about social changes, good or bad. Integrative behaviour must occur mutually if it occurs at all. As Anderson points out, domination induces domination; if two parties to a potential conflict differ markedly in their readiness to be 'integrative' the efforts in that direction by one of them may slightly ease the situation, but a stubbornly dominative attitude in the other will, in the end, make resistance necessary and establish the vicious circle of dominative resistance to attempted domination.

Some people believe that no social aggression is justified, a view which amounts to saying that the development of our capacities for social response is the supreme good. Most people would argue that there are many other equally important values, and it may often be that aggression against certain human beings is the only way of safeguarding some other good thing. When that dilemma occurs we have to make a moral choice. All that psychology can say is that, to the extent that we are social beings, aggression against others is bound to set up conflict within us, and we had better make sure that the purpose for which we violate our social sentiments is important enough to allow us to tolerate the consequent regret.

Nations whose cultures differ widely in the extent and form of social responsiveness that they encourage must meet special difficulties in attempts at amicable co-operation, for they will almost inevitably differ in their attitude to the use of force. One can imagine the difficulties there would be in the way of harmonious negotiation between the suspicious and chronically hostile Dobuans described by Fortune and the friendly and unaggressive Arapesh studied by Mead (1935); the same kind of difficulty, if not the same degree, almost certainly occurs in negotiations between nations whose social responsiveness is not similar in development.

In our present culture a great deal of dominative behaviour (if only in the form of resistance to domination) will be necessary for a long time to come, and among the means of domination open force or the threat of it will remain prominent. Yet it is probably impossible for people who have achieved anything beyond rudimentary social development to resort to the coercion of other people with an easy mind. To use force against others without regret is to reduce them to objects lacking social relevance; lacking relevance, that is, to any sentiment of liking or affection based on a recognition of the intrinsic value to us of social companionship, and the potential value, therefore, of any living being. We all differ in the range and sensitiveness of our social response just as we do in our responsiveness to music or the qualities of wine or the style of a greyhound or anything else. If our social development is rudimentary, we shall feel little or no regret about pugnacity; if it is more advanced we are bound to experience conflict between on the one hand the social sentiment and on the other the intention of using force against the object of the sentiment. The regret that must occur will often become a sense of guilt, sometimes through psychopathological mechanisms, sometimes as a result of the suspicion that we might have managed things without the resort to force.

The problems of sentiment involved in social aggression are illustrated by a journalist's reaction to one of the trials for war crimes after the second German War. Margaret Lane was reviewing (in the London *Evening Standard* of 12th May, 1949) the reports of the Natzweiler trial and expressing what seems to be a very genuine bewilderment. The accused men had been concerned in the execution of four British women agents who, in international law, were spies. The women were not tried, and after long imprisonment they were killed. They were told not that they were going to be killed, but they were to have anti-typhoid injections. In fact, they were given lethal injections and the bodies immediately cremated. The sordid efficiency of the proceedings struck this journalist as revolting, but she also felt a great unreality about the trial of the men concerned in the killings. The prosecution rested on the fact that they had carried out their orders to kill the women, in spite of knowing that there had been no trial and no formal sentence of death against which the women could have appealed. Margaret Lane expressed the uneasy dissatisfaction that many people must feel, knowing that a trial of the women would have led, whether fairly or farcically, to conviction, that no appeal would have succeeded, and that customary methods of execution would have involved more suffering for the victims. Yet she also felt that some protest against the horrible proceedings had rightly been made. She speaks of 'the nightmare feeling that a right fuss is being made for the wrong reason'. What revolts us seems to be the state of mind of the German executioners, for whom human beings have been so reduced in social significance that they can be put to death in the most convenient way without regret or guilt. The rules of war and the rituals of justice exist not only to guard the attacked and the accused from the worst ferocities and from possible injustices; they also have the purpose of guarding fighting men and those concerned with punishment against the guilt induced by engaging in social aggression. Psychologically, the crime of the Natzweiler defendants was that they had made no demand for orthodox safeguards against guilt while they carried out the most extreme form of social aggression.

The extent to which our social responsiveness with its associated sentiments is developed, and the directions in which we are specially sensitive or relatively obtuse, will depend on individual history and on cultural influences and institutions. Social sentiments towards other people may be only one form of a broader and vaguer affection for a wide range of living beings. We may shrink from eating bacon made from a pig that we originally kept for that very purpose; we may refuse to eat any meat from a slaughtered animal; we may be the sort of person who couldn't hurt a fly. It will always be hard to decide, in the absence of deep psychological exploration, whether such sentiments represent a development that is intrinsically satisfying to the individual or whether they are morbid formations resulting from mechanisms of projection and identification. The novelist Ouida (Ffrench, 1938) in her childhood used to bring home a stone that she had picked up in the road, and call it a poor, neglected, unloved thing, and lavish attention and affection on it. Her passionate crusading in her later life against cruelty to animals clearly had threads for the psychopathologist to disentangle. On the other hand, Peter Fleming (1936) tells of some Mongol tribesmen who managed to break the leg of a deer with a lucky rifle shot, and then spent a considerable time jubilantly driving it about on its three legs and generally tormenting it before they killed it. His dislike of that treatment I should suppose not to be morbid, though socially influenced. In our own group at the present time there is a tendency to be suspicious of the whole psychological mechanism of pugnacity on account of the evil uses to which it can be put; we are so concerned with its manifestation in destructiveness and unnecessary attack that we may overlook its other manifestation as vigorous action which modifies the environment in the service of the organism's needs. It seems evident that combativeness is continuous with that self-assertion which is necessary for securing the satisfaction of one's needs and for defining oneself as the unique being which everyone is.

It is perhaps necessary to pay special attention to the type of aggression which looks as if it gave satisfaction in itself or for the pain and destruction it causes, rather than being simply a means to secure some end which the aggressor believes to be otherwise unattainable. Aggression that appears to be an end in itself is very much the concern of psychopathology; and, of course, psychotherapeutic exploration commonly shows that this seemingly autonomous aggression is not after all an end in itself, but serves other hidden ends, whether to give assurance of one's power, to revenge a rebuff, to protest against a frustration or whatever it may be. In spite of some Freudian doctrines to the contrary, it seems likely that all impulses to attack are contingent—contingent on obstruction to the full satisfaction of another desire or on the individual's judgement that some existing satisfaction (including his sense of security) is threatened. This general viewpoint has recently been examined carefully by McKellar (1950), and of course in modern psychology goes back at least as far as McDougall's formulation in 1908, in which, speaking of 'the instinct of pugnacity', he says:

'The condition of its excitement is . . . any opposition to the free exercise of any impulse, any obstruction of the activity to which the creature is impelled by any one of the other instincts. And its impulse is to break down any such obstruction and to destroy whatever offers this opposition' (McDougall, 1908).

There is one difficulty about the view that pugnacity is contingent. The broad pattern of behaviour involved in attack is largely inborn; it is part of the psychophysical inheritance of each species. As Woodworth (1918) suggests, when we possess a bit of behavioural machinery there seems usually to be some satisfaction in using it. Consequently, it seems certain that an animal which can fight will find satisfaction in exercising its skill and power as a fighter; and pugnacity does to that extent become functionally or motivationally autonomous. In human society, that kind of combativeness has been strictly institutionalised in physical games and partly institutionalised in various forms of controversy and debate, and in such regulated abuse as the old Scottish flytings and the contemporary Negro slanging matches called 'playing the dozens' (Golightly and Scheffler, 1948). Among other animals, too, especially but not exclusively among the young, friendly and non-hurtful combat provides the satisfaction of using the machinery of aggression, at a time when the animal has no need to use it against enemies or prey. The characteristic of this kind of combat is the overriding relationship of amity between the contestants (at least, in their overt intention when they start). The fact that we enjoy using the skills of combat gives no support to the view that we all have an inborn urge to hostility and destructiveness which must come out in some form or another. If we were not capable of destroying we couldn't live, but the amount of destruction we actually carry out will be contingent on circumstances.

This relatively simple psychological situation is complicated by one or two possible causes of confusion. The first is that, besides aggression or pugnacity as a pattern of actual response to an environment that needs modifying, there is also aggressiveness as a mood or as a temperamental quality or a personality trait. This, of course, is not the response itself but the disposition to resort to the aggressive response rather easily. The term temperamental quality can most conveniently be used for a supposedly inborn (and in part, presumably, an endocrinally induced) disposition that may show up in any field of activity; it is widely generalised, and our way of working, our love-making, our attack on a problem, our social relations, our way of brushing our teeth may all reveal it. Aggressiveness or assertiveness as a temperamental quality in this broad sense must be closely allied to general vigour of response (though not necessarily to persistence). The term 'personality trait' describes a disposition for one emotion (or attitude) to emerge more readily than others, not over the whole range of our activity but over rather a large area. The personality traits of suspiciousness, for instance, surliness, or touchiness, affect our behaviour towards a wide range of objects and situations, mainly social, but not towards all. Such personality traits may be to a great extent acquired through individual experience. It must often be the task of psychotherapy to modify a personality trait of undue aggressiveness without interfering with the capacity for aggressive action on appropriate occasions.

Seeming differences in aggressiveness as a personality trait are sometimes only differences in the degree of directness with which pugnacity is expressed—whether, for instance, one makes an open row at a committee meeting or embarks on a devious and slower undermining of an opponent. The hostile intention is the same even though a long causal chain intervenes between one's immediate action and the final goal. Recognising this fact of hostile intention lets us out of a difficulty that troubles some psychologists when war is regarded as a form of pugnacious behaviour for the majority of the belligerent population. It is clear that most people in a warring nation are engaged in placid industrial and clerical occupations that provide no direct release for aggressive impulses. In the sections of an ordnance factory where the most sensitive explosives are handled the atmosphere, far from suggesting violence, is more like that of a solemn religious service, and in wartime government departments the only note of ferocity is sounded by the mutual antagonism of rival careerists. But the hope of damaging the national enemy gives meaning, more vividly or less, to all the ordinary occupations, and it links up diverse attitudes and emotions in a causal chain of hostile intention. In the same way, we might be engaged in the idyllic occupation of searching the bed of a brook for smooth stones to use in a sling; our actual experiences would be of alert interest and hope, and then pleasure when we saw the right stone, but they would all be organised within the aggressive intention of killing Goliath or whatever enemy we had in mind. The hostile intention must be recognised as an aspect of aggressive behaviour even in the absence of any experience of anger or any simple expression of pugnacity.

The diversity of expression that a hostile intention may find has become a feature of international affairs, and the old naïve distinction between war and peace has given way to the possibility of non-belligerence, wars of nerves, economic blockades, assaults by propaganda, and cold wars. This development makes it even more evident than before that international hostility is psychologically continuous with the hostility of individual people towards each other, even though the latter is more restricted in expression by the forces of law and group opinion. We cannot plausibly treat war as a psychologically isolated problem. In practice every effort is worth while to limit the amount of actual bombing and shooting; in theory, that kind of war is only the high-light of a wider psychological problem. Psychologically, the antagonism between nations is continuous with the antagonism between workers and employers, teachers and pupils, children and parents within each nation. The connection between personal aggression and war is probably less direct than some psycho-analytic writers (e.g. Glover, 1933, or Durbin and Bowlby, 1939) have implied, and obviously very great weight must be given to the machinery of propaganda and State coercion that brings about the acquiescence of the public in any particular war. Yet it seems clear that war as a social institution could have arisen only among people who had accepted the idea of dominating their fellows in order to achieve some other end.

3

SOCIAL DEVELOPMENT IN EARLY LIFE

It is a commonplace that the family provides a child with its first knowledge of social possibilities and helps to shape its later social development. What the last thirty years of psychological work have disclosed is the unexpected extent and subtlety of early influences, their enduring character, and something of the way in which they work. On this topic there has been a convergence of evidence from clinical psychology, child psychology, anthropology and animal psychology.

Out of many clinical interpretations of the influence of early life, the work of Suttie (1935), which deviates from the Freudian view although deriving from it, seems to offer some of the most convincing insights. Suttie imagines the days of very early infancy to be a relatively blissful period on account of the full emotional rapport between the infant and the mother. True, we can easily overrate the perfection of this 'golden age'; it can hardly be unflawed and later work such as that of Winnicott (1948) and Middlemore (1941) emphasises the importance of psychological strains that may develop in the earliest contacts of mother and child. Yet in reasonably fortunate circumstances it probably offers an easier and a more secure satisfaction of social needs, in the rudimentary form they then possess, than any later period of life.

The early, very easy social relation has to be modified in three chief ways. First, the mother's completely approving love gradually becomes conditional on the infant's behaviour; for instance, on the way it suckles, the amount it cries, its acceptance of toilet training. Secondly, the infant has to learn that the mother is interested in other things besides himself and may sometimes withhold her attention in favour of some other concern. Thirdly, he must learn that the mother is fond of other people as well as himself. In favourable circumstances, the tension set up in these ways can be tolerated fairly easily because new possibilities of satisfaction present themselves as the earlier indulgences are withdrawn; the conditional love is secured by efforts of control that are not beyond the maturing infant's capacity; as the mother's exclusive attention is more and more sacrificed, so the infant can begin to discover the satisfaction of sharing with her an interest in things outside them both; and with the loss of what had seemed her exclusive affection there develop contacts with an increasing number of creatures, father, brothers, sisters, to whom the child can look for social responsiveness and affection. From early days the growing infant is thus initiated into three broad features of social life, individual activities carried out with social sanction, interests shared with those around him, and a place within a network of companionship.

Modern psychotherapy has largely been concerned with unravelling the effects on adult behaviour and outlook of individual differences of experience during these phases of development. There seems no doubt that ingrained expectations about social life and established modes of adjustment to other people can usually be traced back a very long way into early childhood. In its more obvious expressions we take this principle as a matter of course; we expect, for instance, that a man's persistently bad relations with people in authority will be found not only to run through his contacts with employers, officers and teachers, but to go back to some unsatisfactory experience of parental authority, or its lack. The same unwitting use of the family pattern as a paradigm for later social behaviour can be seen in less obvious but not less important ways. One notices the girl who expects, all through life, to wheedle her own way with men in authority but knows that women in authority must be either obeyed or defied; the people whose sibling jealousy makes it hard for them to tolerate the fact that their friends have other friends; those who find difficulty in accepting help because from their earliest days help savoured too much of interference; those whose early uncertainty about the dependability of their parents' justice leads them constantly to crave some completely just authority who will measure out reward and punishment where they are really deserved. Innumerable expectations and attitudes, firmly established though often quite unwitting, can be shown to have a continuity with persistent features of very early experience. It is fortunate that valuable expectations and habits of mind, equally with disabling ones, may be lastingly induced by persistent good features of upbringing.

Though the very enduring effect of early experience is nowadays commonly accepted as a fact, the explanation of it receives less attention than it deserves. Why, after all, should the social experience of early childhood have so lasting an effect when it is overlaid with a vastly greater volume of other, and often contrasting, experiences in the wider social contacts of schooldays and adult life? To speak of early 'malleability', to say that as the twig is bent so the tree will grow, is to use metaphors that tell us nothing about the psychological processes involved.

Several different causes probably contribute to the disproportionate effectiveness of early experience. One is that, because we are always combining present with past experience, the growing child is likely to attend selectively to those features of the wider social world that confirm his expectations. It is true that he will meet experiences that challenge his expectations and may in the end modify his outlook, but they work at a disadvantage because he is inclined to regard them as anomalous. The authoritarian father, for instance, will be reflected in a certain number of domineering teachers and bosses, and although the child will find other types of teacher and boss he will tend to think of them as exceptions and will cling to his stereotype of the authoritarian boss. Or again, if an anxious mother has always urged him on to the next achievement and the next difficulty before he has enjoyed the security of having overcome the last, he will find some teachers who do the same, and for him they will be the 'real' teachers and the others will be exceptions. The early expectations are largely unconscious and will persist for a very long while in spite of conflicting experiences at the conscious level.

B

Another reason for the lasting influence of childhood experience is that by our expectations we actually modify our social environment. The consistently abject person does in the end get treated with disdain. Ruth Washburn (1932) reported on two girls of the same age and almost identical upbringing who were observed systematically when introduced to a playroom and left with other children. They were first seen at ten months and the observations went on periodically until they were ten years old. Over the whole period there was a consistent difference between the two: X was socially confident, Y was withdrawn; Y was insecure, distrustful of other children and distrustful of her own capacities in any unfamiliar situation; although she wanted to play as the other children did, she only looked on, and not until she got home and felt secure again would she imitate their play. Still more important from the present point of view, it was observed that just as she made few approaches to the other children, in contrast to X who was forthcoming, so after a time the others gave up trying to approach her. It is perfectly clear that in this way two such contrasting children, although in the same objective social world, are in fact creating each for herself a sharply different social environment and one which is self-perpetuating.

Finally, it seems possible that the happenings of early life gain in impressiveness from the relative fewness of landmarks in the infant's experience; there is not then a multiplicity of events to fill his days and compete with each other for attention and emotional response. In later life the effectiveness of any event is fairly rapidly modified by the bombardment of succeeding impressions. It is, moreover, often damped down from the start by devices of repression, distraction and emotional withdrawal; or it is distanced by being put into the perspective of similar experiences (after the fashion of the Greek chorus putting the calamity of the moment into the long catalogue of misfortunes of the same kind). Even the things that happen in later childhood and remain in memory often strike us as having filled the whole mental horizon in a way that can be matched only by exceptionally intense and important experiences in later life.

A full explanation of the lasting effects of early experiences is no doubt still to be sought. The fact itself, emphasised mainly by psychotherapists, has recently received support from animal psychology in the work of Hunt and others (1947) which has been confirmed in general by Albino and Long (1951). Hunt and his collaborators based their experiment on the fact that rats have a disposition to hoard food over and above what they need to eat. They subjected litters of young rats, just after weaning, to rather severe experiences of partial starvation; they then restored them to a normal diet until they had recovered physically (i.e. had caught up in weight with a control group): finally, they compared the hoarding of these rats in adult life with the hoarding of a control group of rats that had not experienced food deprivation in early life. The results were that there was no difference between the two groups when food supplies were adequate and all the rats were satiated, but when three days of partial starvation were inflicted on both groups and their immediately subsequent hoarding observed, the rats that had been starved in infancy now (on this 'reminder' of starvation) hoarded on the average more than the others. There were great individual differences among the animals, some who had not been starved in infancy hoarding more than some who had; but the differences in the average of the two groups' behaviour provides support for the general principle that very early experience is likely to have a disproportionate influence on later psychological characteristics.

The absence of any differences between the two groups until adult experience had brought a 'reminder' of the past (to use a metaphor for whatever process reactivated the past experience) is consistent with the view of several modern psychotherapists (e.g. Horney, 1937) that the events of early life are not in themselves decisive in determining later attitudes; they are effective only if later experiences give at least some confirmation of the attitudes they engendered. This principle is, of course, entirely compatible with the view that very early experience is proportionately more formative than later.

The same principle is given profuse illustration in the studies of the 'culture-pattern' school of anthropologists. Here the focus changes. Where the clinical psychologists have concentrated on the effects of individual differences in upbringing within the same culture, the anthropologists have shown that broad similarities of child-handling within any one culture help to perpetuate the characteristic features of adult behaviour and outlook that distinguish one culture from another. Bateson and Mead's account of the upbringing of the Balinese, for example, has already been referred to; it shows convincingly that the withdrawn and over-detached manner of the adults arises from techniques of child-rearing. Similar detailed studies among other Pacific peoples and some of the Indian peoples of the south-west of the United States (cf. du Bois, 1944, and Leighton and Kluckhohn, 1948) point in the same direction. Speculative extensions of the theme to complex societies have been attempted for the Japanese (Benedict, 1947) and the Russians (Gorer and Rickman, 1949). Sceptical caution is clearly necessary in the whole area (cf. Orlansky, 1949), but a survey of evidence by Whiting and Child (1953) demonstrates a relation between child-rearing practices and at least some features of adult outlook. Grygier (1951) suggests that the practices themselves matter less than the attitudes they express. He claims that the effects of close swaddling in babyhood were different in Russians and Poles: Russian mothers followed the custom because they thought of the infant's strength as being potentially dangerous to itself and making it difficult to handle, but Polish mothers justified it in terms of the infant's great fragility; and as a result they apparently induced less rage in the infant. It would seem that the physical techniques adopted are of psychological importance largely because of psychological attitudes in the parents to which they are an index, a fact that helps to explain some of the pathetic futilities of the methods of child-rearing attempted by western parents in the early years of Freudian influence.

All of these studies serve to illustrate the coherence that must exist between, on the one hand, adult institutions and outlook and, on the other, attitudes that have been inculcated, sometimes deliberately and sometimes without thought of consequences, in very young children. This mutual reinforcement between the family and the wider institutions of the group is to be expected; it is clear, for instance, that German and Japanese views on discipline and on the relative status of men and women are almost certain to be expressed in the early upbringing of boys and girls. Without this mutual reinforcement, a culture could not continue as a coherent whole. And this serves as a reminder that deep-going reforms and changes of outlook cannot be stabilised in a society until a large proportion of a new generation has grown up with the new outlook from very early in life.

Development as a social individual is a long process, one that obviously need not stop when physical maturity is reached. Some psychological studies have already been made of the social development of children, both in primitive societies (e.g. Mead, 1929) and in complex western societies (e.g. Piaget, 1932 and Isaacs, 1933), but there is no doubt that much more remains to be done. The comparative study of cultures, in this respect as in others, gives invaluable hints for more intensive studies of aspects of our own culture that might otherwise be taken for granted.

Margaret Mead's study of girls in Samoa, for instance, focused attention on the institutions and culturally induced attitudes that contribute largely to the strains experienced by adolescent girls in our own society. The wider diffusion, in Samoan society, of the sources both of affection and of authority seemed to her to make for an easier transition from childhood to womanhood, and whether or not her interpretations were sound at all points it seems clear that the study of a primitive society enabled her to criticise more decisively an aspect of her own culture that might otherwise have seemed to be the inevitable outcome of biological facts.

Less well known is the useful descriptive account by W. S. Taylor (1948) of the orthodox Hindu culture pattern, now obsolescent. He draws attention to the fact that the young Hindu child is subjected to strict discipline only in matters arising out of the caste system and its associated taboos, a segment of life in which the parents are under as strict a discipline as that which they impose. The result, he thinks, is to give the child from a very early age the clear notion of a supra-parental source of authority, child and parents being united in obedience to it. The close psychological association of parents and children is enhanced by the relative absence of toys and games that segregate the various age levels from each other; instead, children of all ages play together, and from a very early age the child finds satisfying pursuits in helping the parents in their occupational tasks. In this respect, it sounds as though the orthodox Hindu family developed, and extended to boys as well as girls, the fairly close association of child and parent that we often find between a middle-class girl and her mother. At these points, such a study of a contrasting culture invites us to look more closely at the causes and effects of our own sharper divisions between age levels.

The outcome of some of the western traditions and customary outlooks connected with authority and the source of moral obligation is seen in the illuminating study of Swiss children made by Piaget (1932). His work has been criticised for some defects of experimental method and for a tendency to imply stages of development that are more clear-cut than the facts warrant, but no one seems to have shown that his broad conclusions are far astray.

He centred his study of children's social development round inquiries into their attitude to the rules of games (such as marbles) and the judgements they gave about the relative naughtiness of childish misdeeds that were related to them, the fairness of punishments and the justice of various examples of sharing among children. The study of the rules of games had the advantage of being more concrete; the other inquiries depended on the children's understanding of stories and their readiness to express their opinions verbally.

From the results of his study, Piaget distinguishes successive stages in the child's social development which correspond on the average with chronological age. He admits that there is much overlap between the stages, and it is obvious that individual differences may cause wide deviations from the scheme he suggests. Moreover, as he says, his findings concern children in the poorer parts of Geneva and might not be applicable to children of different social strata or different localities. But the general trend that he observes seems convincing. He notes first the purely motor and individual activity of the very young child (of, say, two or three years old) who may play with marbles simply as objects to be pushed about, dropped, poured into the indentations of upholstery, etc. A little later comes the 'egocentric' stage when the child knows of the existence of codified rules and makes a show of imitating them, but in fact still plays a game by himself, or, if in the presence of other children, without trying to win or to integrate his activities with the others; at this stage (which is at its height in the fourth to sixth years) everyone in the game can win at once.

The next stage is that of 'incipient co-operation'. Here each child playing marbles tries to win and is, therefore, concerned with mutual control and unified rules. But his grasp of the rules is still uncertain and children of seven or eight who are in the same class at school and constantly play together will still give contradictory accounts of the rules when questioned separately. Round about the age of eleven (with wide deviations on either side) there appears the stage of what Piaget calls 'the codification of rules', in which there is close agreement in the information given by all the children of the same class at school, with great elaboration of the rules and special provisions for every conceivable turn the game may take. Boys at this stage (but not girls, or not to anything like the same extent) seem to find a dominating interest in the rules themselves.

Side by side with this development in the understanding of the rules, there comes a change of attitude towards their binding force and a changing view of the authority from which it is derived. In the earliest stages, of course, no sense of obligation exists. There appears a second stage (lasting from the height of the egocentric phase to the first half of the co-operative phase) in which the rules are regarded as sacred and untouchable, emanating from adults and lasting for ever, any alteration of them being a transgression. And yet this exaggerated respect for the almost divine code of rules is found to go hand in hand with 'egocentric' practices that seriously infringe the rules. Finally there appears a third stage in which a rule is seen to derive its authority only from the mutual consent of the players, and an alteration of the rules is perfectly permissible if general consent can be secured. This stage is reached at about the age of ten and from then on the rules of the game of marbles are really obeyed. If at this stage differences of opinion arise as to the details of a rule, no appeal to external authority is possible, but the disagreement has to be adjusted within the group of players themselves.

The essence of Piaget's work along these lines was to show that the child passed gradually from a stage where adult authority, externally imposed, seemed the only source of moral control, to a stage where the children felt that their group had moral autonomy and where they submitted to an authority derived from mutual consent. In his further studies of the children's verbal judgements on justice, punishment and sharing he showed similarly a process by which the child gradually freed itself from the merely constraining authority of grown-ups or older children, passed through a stage in which strictly equal treatment for every child regardless of circumstances was insisted on, and finally reached a phase where a more complex 'equity' was required, with special allowances for younger children, the unfortunate, the tired, and so on. However much Piaget's detailed interpretations may be questioned, his work seems to show convincingly that, in the culture in which he worked, social development involves a gradual detachment from the constraint of parental and quasi-parental authority and an acceptance in their place of personally discovered obligations deriving from the necessity of mutual adjustment between equal companions.

Another line of work concerned with the socialisation of children is represented by efforts to measure 'emotional maturity', efforts that are characteristic of one kind of psychology in attempting to derive a numerical measure of a personal quality from paper-and-pencil tests. Most of them (e.g. Furfey, 1935, and Pressey, 1933) work by determining for each year of childhood an average set of interests, hobby preferences, fears, worries, sources of guilt, admired traits of character and so on, and then measuring the individual child against the average of his age. Rough as they are, these tests can be of use in some limited situations. Their fundamental limitation lies in their criterion of 'maturity'. It amounts simply to what is current among children of a given social group at a given period. All that the tests measure is the child's increasing conformity to the sophistication of the average young adult in the particular community, and it is hard to think of anything much more lacking in general interest. The scale of emotional maturity devised by Willoughby (1932) is of rather greater interest since it is based, even if in a muddled way, on some standards of social maturity. They derive from psycho-analytic work, and the only argument for the scale's validity is the circular one that a hundred judges who accepted the broad principles of psycho-analysis could agree with it. Among its implied criteria of maturity, those which would be widely accepted in our culture include a decreasing absorption in oneself, increasing self-reliance, and freedom from compulsive competition with others and from demands for deference. Further work along the same lines might well be done with the more systematic guidance of a book such as Flugel's *Man, Morals and Society* (1945), which in effect offers an ethical system derived from (or, as some aver, translated into terms of) psycho-analysis.

The fact is that as soon as the later phases of social development are considered it grows obvious that we are dealing in general with the scale of values accepted by one social group at one period of its history, and in particular with the sort of relation to other people that it regards as desirable and the importance it attaches to achieving that relation as compared with attaining other desirable ends. Psychological inquiry into the problem has not gone far, and it is still disputable what contribution psychology could hope to make.

In practice it will almost certainly affect our appraisal of various possibilities of social life because it demonstrates the circumstances of culture and upbringing that have induced particular types of social response. The schizoid withdrawal of the Balinese, for instance, has to be judged as something gratuitously and artificially induced. Again Suttie (1935) shows how the sham 'toughness' that was fashionable between the wars (and helped to make the vogues of Hemingway and Dashiell Hammett at their respective levels) is induced in the growing child by a mother who is over-dependent on his infantile attachment to her and so creates difficulties in his psychological weaning. And, in the same way, such traits as exhibitionism, narcissism, compulsive competitiveness, extreme distrust, are commonly traced to particular circumstances of upbringing. This in itself settles no ethical question (for some artificially induced things are valuable). But it alters the psychological status of the resultant trait and, supposing we dislike it, gives us the assurance that it can be modified, that it is not the outcome of unchanging biological or psychological facts. It tends to free our range of ethical choice from the chains of a particular culture.

Whether this kind of psychological inquiry has a converse in the positive implication that some forms of social development are more 'natural' than others has been given remarkably little attention. The very question would be derided by many psychologists who believe that the 'human nature' common to all cultures is not worth serious study; but the signs are that others are coming to consider it more seriously.

At present one can only indicate with reasonable confidence some of the broad trends in the development of sociability that our own culture accepts as normal. The basic impulse to value other people is expressed first in the infant's attachment to the mother, who is the source of satisfaction for this as for all other impulses. The basic need is thus canalised at once into a rudimentary sentiment. As the child grows, similar though less exclusive sentiments form around other people, and around the habits and things and places associated with them. At the same time, the growing child develops personality traits concerned with other people: trust, distrust, quarrelsomeness, generosity, docility, co-operativeness, competitiveness, and so on, all affected greatly by individual upbringing but usually compassed within a broad range that differs from (though partly overlapping) the range found in other cultures.

In general, one can rightly speak of the widening circle of people from whom the socially developing child derives the satisfaction of being liked and valued, but this widening does not go on indefinitely. For one thing, various phases of experience bring sharp refocusings of social desire on to one or a few people: falling in love, for instance, or developing a close friendship, or becoming devoted to one's children. Differences in the strength of the innumerable sentiments that contribute to our social satisfaction are regarded as normal among us. There are, of course, wide individual differences in the range of people with whom we can find acceptable companionship; but not even the most extreme extravert is entirely promiscuous in his sociability. The individual's effort after acceptable companionship is a clue to the understanding of many features of social organisation.

Note. Some of the most interesting work of the 1950s and 1960s across the borderline between animal and human psychology promises further understanding of the lasting effects of early experience. One aspect of the fact itself has gained wide popular recognition through the work of Bowlby (1951) on children deprived of maternal affection. There is some possibility (cf. Bowlby, 1958) that if the ability to form any trustfully affectionate relation with others is to be established easily and effectively, it must be elicited during a rather short critical period of early life. The suggestion arises partly from experience in child psychotherapy and partly by analogy with 'imprinting' in animals, to which Lorenz (1952) vividly drew attention. Other ethologists (cf. Thorpe, 1963) are now extending and refining on the original observations and their theoretical interpretation.

In an allied field of animal psychology Harlow (see Foss (ed.), 1961) has studied other aspects of early social response by depriving infant monkeys of natural mothering and providing them with artificial mother-surrogates of various kinds. He was able to demonstrate the great importance to the infant of contact with a warm soft surface, as distinct from mere nutrition, and he showed that the presence of the mother-surrogate was necessary if the infants were to explore their surroundings freely and play securely. The effects of this substitute-mothering on the monkeys' later development are often disastrous (cf. Harlow & Harlow, 1962).

All this work holds great promise, though with some danger of dividing into two lines—one of over-simplification and plausible speculation, the other of arid concentration on increasingly minute details of response in the species that lend themselves to laboratory experiment.

4

THE INDIVIDUAL'S MORALITY

Some of the interest and value of Piaget's work on moral development comes from his occupying a position midway between psychology and sociology. The difference between the two disciplines gives rise to perennial discussion, mostly sterile, but although the distinction is becoming still more uncertain with the increasing variety of work regarded as sociology and with the growth of some kinds of psychology, yet the modal psychologist remains very different from the modal sociologist. He is usually more concerned with what Blake called the minute particulars, and it is only by groping through these that he approaches generalisations and abstractions. In the early part of his book, Piaget works as a psychologist, his experimental method far from inpeccable but basically sound, revealing something of the behaviour, thinking and sentiments of actual children in particular situations. In the latter part, he turns to sociological theory, very abstract, very generalised, very dependent on the meaning attached to uncertain concepts. 'The sociologist' will feel that in this latter part Piaget is at last coming to the heart of the problem; 'the psychologist' will be bored and dissatisfied, feeling that after a good beginning Piaget has let himself sink back into an armchair furnished with the air-cushioning of polysyllables. Most psychologists would like vastly more empirical observation before generalising about morality, and they would want their eventual generalisations to refer not merely to broadly described social trends but to intimate psychological processes in the individual members of groups.

Much of Piaget's argument is concerned to mark out his areas of agreement and disagreement with Durkheim's theory of morality which derives all sense of moral obligation from a recognition of the authority exercised by society. This would obliterate the distinction that Piaget makes between the obligation imposed by an authority that we accept and the obligation arising from our wish to co-operate with equals. Piaget stresses the serious difficulty that Durkheim faces in explaining on his theory how it comes about that some of the behaviour we regard as most highly moral (that of martyrs, for example) involves defiance of the authority of society, and he is naturally dissatisfied with the sleight of tongue that explains such a case by saying that the martyr is obedient not to society as it appears to itself but to society as it really is or tends to be.

However, Piaget still has to show that his own view will take account more easily of the fact that moral behaviour and conformity to group standards are not the same. There seems no good reason why the wish to co-operate with a pack of equals should not produce as much individual subservience as the wish to obey the elders. Riesman (1950) gives a sobering picture of just such subservience in what he calls the 'other-directed' individual of contemporary America. Piaget's way round the difficulty is to say that, whereas social constraint identifies what is with what ought to be, social co-operation insists only on our consenting to the principle that what we affirm to be desirable should be tried out and tested by others.

The crucial question is what happens when the others disagree. If on further trial we still think we are right, is the 'moral' course to recant or to reaffirm our view? Piaget does not give an answer. If to recant, then it would seem that Piaget's idea of moral behaviour is in the last resort obligatory conformity to the group, though he hopes that there will be much give and take before that ultimate authority is invoked. If the moral course is to go our way, like the martyrs, and also like the obstinate cranks, then the sanction for what we do would seem to lie within us as social individuals, a possibility that Piaget appears to follow Durkheim in dismissing at the outset.

Yet this dilemma of abstractions is not something that arises from the observations on children's behaviour recorded in the first part of the book. There, of course, one saw the immense importance of social influences in guiding the child's preference for one kind of action rather than another, and the gradual change in those social influences, so that the earlier exclusive authority of elders was modified by the authority of a group, of which the child was a more or less equal co-operating member. Piaget saw this as a progress towards what he calls an autonomous conscience. In spite of using this term, however, he avoids any recognition that the individual approaches a point where, when problems of behaviour arise, he takes responsibility for his own decisions, with or without the approval of his group and without dependence on any way of thinking that it happens to sanction. And yet Piaget gives examples from the children's behaviour of this individual autonomy in the choice of a course of action. Asking children what they do if another child punches them, he found from nine onwards (up to twelve) a big majority in favour of punching back, and among the boys a majority who believed in giving back exactly the same number of blows as they had received. (The figures he gives are lamentably inadequate, consisting of percentages without an indication of the number of cases, but one hopes that the very broad trend is reliable.) But there were individual children (especially, it would appear, among the girls) who saw beyond this principle of simple reciprocity. Many girls believed in giving back fewer blows than they had received; one of them, ten years old, said, 'I hit him back less, because if I hit him back the same or more, he begins again.' A boy of ten objected to revenge because 'there is no end' to it.

The natural view of these reasonable children's answers would be to say that through experience they had decided for themselves that their age-group's simple code of tit-for-tat was unsatisfactory and that, perhaps with the sole authority of their own experience, they had abandoned it. Piaget tries instead to argue that it is really a concern for social reciprocity which has led them to this position; what they regard as just, he says, 'is no longer merely reciprocal action but primarily behaviour that admits of indefinitely sustained reciprocity'. And yet it is the possibility of this 'indefinitely sustained reciprocity', of tit-for-tat, that the ten-year-old boy objects to because there is no end to it. Here Piaget, in a curious parallel to Durkheim's device of distinguishing between society as it appears to itself and as it really is or tends to be, is reduced to saying that 'reciprocity has two aspects: reciprocity as a fact and reciprocity as an ideal, as something which ought to be'; and he sees the children who have got beyond tit-for-tat as practising the latter. This seems to be an effort to sustain a preconceived theory rather than to systematise the observed facts.

The central doubt is whether we need constantly refer to the individual's social allegiance in explaining the code of behaviour that he accepts. Admittedly his concern with standards of behaviour at all will depend largely on psychological developments that could not have occurred without the aid of a social context, but so equally will all his more advanced concerns, his structure of preferences in visual design or music for instance. It is obvious that our account of individual advances in the creation and enjoyment of music or design would be hampered if we felt obliged constantly to explain them as an indirect attempt to conform to common taste sanctioned by society, if not society as it appears to itself then society as it really is or tends to be, or if not common taste as a fact then common taste as an ideal. So, too, with creative individual advances in standards of behaviour. We are hamstrung from the start if we suppose that their value must be derived in some devious way from the authority of the social group, which in all probability they have to defy.

It seems safer to start from the patent fact that although much of the behaviour we admire has involved conformity to the standards of a social group some of it has not, including some which has been most sensitive to the value of other human beings. The growth of a person, simultaneously as an individual and a social being, does for a time show itself in a gradually increasing conformity to the adult standards of a social group. But it would be disastrous to assume that those standards must continue to be the measure of development. Group conformity and social development may in the early years of life be closely connected and perhaps difficult to distinguish. But a dissociation of the two ideas (to use Remy de

Gourmont's phrase) is of the utmost importance in understanding the continued social development of the more mature members of a group; and we have to think of social development as compatible with increasing individual diversities, and with an independent individual assay of group values which stands far apart from conformity in the ordinary sense.

In examining this possibility, we have a useful lead in the work of Trotter (1916) who made a distinction between the 'resistive' and the 'sensitive', the former being that large majority who 'resist' their own experience (by repression, rationalisation and re-interpretation of all kinds) whenever a clear recognition of it would bring them into conflict with the values and outlook of their group. The 'sensitive' are those who take their own experiences seriously even when it clashes with the conventional outlook. The distinction is no doubt one of degree; there are not two 'types'. Its importance for the present purpose lies in the fact, clearly implied by Trotter, that the 'sensitive' are not lacking in social impulse; in fact, he suggests that they contribute more than the 'resistive' to the development of altruistic sentiments. They may be less gregarious but they are not less social.

Our understanding of what is called moral behaviour will be relatively clumsy if we neglect the differences associated with the individual's degree of 'sensitiveness' in this special sense. It affects two broad questions with which psychology must be concerned: first, the question of where we get our standards, how we build up the ordered structure of sentiments with which, in so far as we behave morally, we harmonise our actions; second, the question why we do try to behave morally.

It goes without saying that everyone's scale of values is immensely influenced by the traditions and the customary outlook of his social group. In recent years this has been demonstrated with vivid examples and in great detail by social anthropologists such as Benedict (1935), Mead (1935), Linton (1947), du Bois (1944) and Thompson (1950), who have also done a great deal to show through what social processes the group's outlook may be inculcated in children. But the general fact of variation in moral standards from group to group has long been common knowledge (cf. the systematic study of its ethical implications by Westermarck, 1932); McDougall, for example, saw clearly that the detailed behaviour expressing what he called 'instincts' (or 'propensities') might differ widely in different cultures.

The work of the social anthropologists confirms the other common observation that, although the culture of a group shapes all its members in broadly the same way it still leaves individual differences and a certain number of sharp deviations from the usual pattern. There always have been people who differed widely from their social group in evaluating one or other aspect of their experience, and their deviant standards of value have often been justifiable —at any rate, to the extent that most of our conduct is—on conscious, rational grounds. They have certainly not always diverged in the direction of delinquency, iconoclasm or a mere slackening of standards. The more seriously an individual takes his experience (to use Trotter's concept) the more important it is for him to put the conventional values of his group to the test of individual experience. True, he need not commit murder in order to see whether it conflicts with his own sentiments, but he can take his experience of anger and hatred seriously and discover to what extent his destructive and pugnacious impulses are out of harmony with other features of his personality. He may or may not find that his experience confirms the established values of his group. Because some psychologists still speak as if the unregenerate individual grew moral simply by yielding to social pressure, it becomes important to emphasise the equally significant cases in which he resists it in order to be moral. Martyrdom and conscientious objection may provide the dramatic illustrations, but the same principle holds on innumerable occasions of everyday life. It is not invalidated by the fact that much eccentricity is worthless and that even the valuable deviations frequently grow from roots that are in part neurotic.

The implication is that in some degree the social individual creates standards for himself. The psychological question is how he does this. (The question of what it ultimately means in terms of ethics is not at issue here.) It is, of course, readily agreed that some standards for the guidance of conduct are established by trial and choice. The individual discovers that eating too much cake and jelly makes him feel ill, and he ultimately controls the impulse or regards it as a lapse if he fails to. It is sometimes supposed that this principle can lead to the guidance of action only in the interest of selfish ends and not to the consideration for others that forms a part of most codes of behaviour and feeling. The objection ignores the fact that we are—and probably are by nature—social beings and that we like other people; their satisfaction and happiness are of direct value to us, and acts of ours which spoil them conflict with one of the strongest systems of sentiment that we possess. The vast implications of this simple fact that most of us like other people has often been strangely neglected in discussions of moral behaviour. Psychologically it is no matter for surprise that the test of individual experience and preference should confirm moral codes that place a high value on consideration for others. There seems no reason to doubt that all features of a group's code of behaviour may be tested, and either confirmed or resisted, by the individual; and consequently that not only immoral but highly moral behaviour may bring a man into conflict with his group.

One aspect of this fact has been clearly recognised, perhaps exaggerated. Many writers suggest that the corporate behaviour of organised groups, notably nations, is morally inferior to that of the individuals composing them. Ginsberg (1947), after noting that private citizens now recognise that they share moral responsibility for what their state does, goes on to suggest that 'confusion arises when the ordinary man realises that on behalf of their state men are expected to do acts which in the sphere of private relations they would regard as monstrous'.

The question is of some complexity. To see the issue clearly one must in the first place exclude actions which, immoral in ordinary contexts, are (rightly or wrongly) re-interpreted and given a different moral significance by means of some institution. The deliberate killing of others, which in private is murder, is morally re-interpreted by such social institutions as war, capital punishment and vendetta. The woman who fills detonators for shells and bombs is in a totally different psychological state from the woman who helps her lover to kill her husband. While the individual accepts a social institution the psychological significance of an act committed within the institutional framework is different from that of the same act committed outside it.

Some important moral changes come about through the refusal of individuals to accept the institutional re-interpretation of certain acts. The slave trade was abolished because deviant individuals thought that human capture and slavery were abhorrent, and resisted the view (which claimed Biblical support) that these things were unobjectionable if the victims were black. Cruelty to animals has gradually been perceived in one practice after another (of sport, trade and agriculture) which has previously received institutional re-interpretation; in this country biting the head off a plucked sparrow fluttering in a hat was once an acceptable sport; the present position of fox-hunting shows an institution on the defensive against those who see cruelty in the acts for which it supplies re-interpretations. So, too, in the nineteen-twenties there was an effort to see sexual promiscuity in the same light for men and women and to deny re-interpretations in terms of the double code. Human sacrifice, duelling, the vendetta, capital punishment and war are all institutions whose special interpretation of the act of killing has been challenged by individuals; and the present institution of permitting conscientious objection recognises the possibility that for some deviant individuals the social re-interpretation of killing in warfare may genuinely have failed.

It remains evident, however, that while individual people can accept such institutions of their group they cannot feel guilty about what they do. The act they were asked to do on behalf of their state is not psychologically the same act that they would recoil from in private life.

A second fallacy in the over-facile contrast of private and public morality consists in comparing acts that are not true parallels psychologically. Admittedly, the ambassador who lies abroad for the good of his country would probably not tell lies about his laundry losses; but if, for instance, he knew of a friend's marital infidelity and was asked for evidence that would reach the friend's wife, he might then lie, with the same argument as he would use in his public life—that a lie would on balance do more good than harm. For a true comparison equally complex moral situations must be chosen. The dispute over the Lane Bequest illustrates this point. Sir Hugh Lane wished to give his pictures to the National Gallery of Ireland on condition that they were properly housed. He thought the condition was not fulfilled and sent the pictures on loan to the National Gallery, London, bequeathing them to that Gallery by his will of 1913. In 1915 he added a codicil revoking the bequest and giving thirty-nine pictures to Ireland again, on condition that they were properly housed within five years of his death.

'Unfortunately, he went down with the *Lusitania* before getting a witness to his signature to that codicil. None disputed its genuineness yet—such meanness is almost incredible—the rich National Gallery of England, taking legal advantage of that omission, stuck to the booty. They were backed by the Government. In private life and individually the Trustees of the National Gallery would never have dreamt of behaving like that' (Reviewer in the *Sunday Times*, 2nd February, 1947).

The implied contrast is with one of the trustees, as a private individual, having to choose between hanging on to the pictures for himself and giving them to the Dublin gallery. But the trustees were responsible to their successors and the nation and were not acting simply for themselves; the comparison should, therefore, be with the trustee in his capacity as, say, the owner of an entailed estate with strong family traditions who could assert (whether or not as a rationalisation) that he was thinking mainly of his family. Suppose, then, that he had the bequest of a small piece of land that would add greatly to the value of his estate, a bequest that was then revoked without legal witness by a man who had had an impulsive reversal of intention in the same matter before. Suppose further, that the estate that would benefit by the codicil was traditionally hostile to the trustee's family and, as a result of the long quarrel, was in acute disorder at the time. In these circumstances it seems altogether likely that even as individuals the trustees would have done just what they did as a corporate body. Naturally the rights and wrongs of the case are not in question here; all that concerns us is that the contrast between private and public morality seems much less evident when cases of similar complexity are compared.

The contrast in fact depends on a much exaggerated notion of private morality. This, in turn, is encouraged by the oversharp contrast we often draw between a criminal minority and the law-abiding, with our tendency to neglect the sub-criminality of everyday life among the unconvicted majority. Minor thefts, especially from large organisations (cf. Waites, 1945), false representation about goods for sale, corruption, malicious damage, cruelty and neglect in dealing with children and animals, are all very common and most of them not confined to any one social or economic stratum. These are not merely offences against governmental regulations but delinquencies by the psychological criterion that in the absence of rationalisation the offenders themselves would feel some guilt about them and would feel shame if they were exposed to an unsympathetic public.

Here one reaches the second broad psychological question, as to why it is that we try to live up to whatever standards of behaviour we possess, whether individually tested or taken without question from the people around us. We can well begin by recognising that if our ethical code is also the code of our group, one elementary reason for obeying it is fear of the penalties (ranging from dislike to physical punishment) that other people will inflict if they detect our delinquency. It would be absurd to underrate the part played by fear of punishment in keeping most of us relatively law-abiding, and responsible psychologists make no such mistake. Mackwood (1949), for instance, reporting on psychotherapeutic work with convicted prisoners, notes the class of ordinary or 'normal' delinquents who have at first got away with their crimes but are pulled up short by their first prison sentence:

'In the group who have been getting away with it the first conviction is often the last. They are convicted, *and convinced*, in Court; the game is not worth the candle.'

For many other people a vivid reminder of the possibility of punishment is enough. Five Post Office workers were sentenced to imprisonment for stealing part of the money they were employed to collect from telephone boxes in south-east London. They alleged that it was a common practice.

'Mr. James Burge, prosecuting, said that since these men had been sus-
pended from duty, collections from the south-east London district had
gone up by about £170 a week' (London *Evening Standard*, 9th January,
1951).

But a little honest introspection is enough to convince most of us
that fear of punishment contributes something towards keeping us
law-abiding.

In most people, however, there is a more important motive for
avoiding crime even when detection is unlikely. A breach of the
moral code that we share with other people automatically deprives
us of our own sense of having group support in what we do: we
know that our group now sanctions us not for what we are but
for what we pretend to be. This penalty is admittedly evaded to a
great extent by rationalisation (e.g. 'It's only what everybody does
but they don't admit it'), but for the more integrated person some
discomfort lingers. At the very least his mental comfort while he
joins in the denunciation of the unrighteous (an important form
of gossip for sustaining the moral standards of groups) will be
flawed when he remembers his own offence.

A third factor, and probably the most important, contributes to
making us obey whatever code we have ourselves accepted, or at
least making us feel guilty if we disobey it. This is simply the
central effort of a living being to remain an integrated whole and
avoid the tension that results from actions conflicting with the
stable features of his personality, such as his sentiments and the
established hierarchy of his values. This is not to overlook the
surprising reconciliation of incompatibles that can be achieved by
rationalisation. But as far as we manage to remain integrated and
to see the clash between our actions and our sentiments about such
actions, we shall experience what we call a sense of guilt, the dis-
agreeable awareness of a disharmony within us that our own actions
have created. The fundamental tendency towards coherent behaviour, in accordance with whatever values we recognise, is a
factor in morality that derives from our nature as biological
individuals and not from our membership of a social group.

The fact seems to be that social groups have been given rather
more significance, favourable or unfavourable, for the individual

person's moral behaviour than they deserve. Genetically the processes of socialisation and moral development go hand in hand for some way, and the work of Piaget traces their joint course. Later they may diverge. The individual's standards may be more consistent and more sensitive to the facts of experience than those of his group, or they may be the reverse. In the service of his group or under its influence he may come nearer to following the principles he accepts or he may fall unusually far below his nominal standards. The degree to which he is sensitive to his own experience, avoiding rationalisation and declining the re-interpretation which social convention offers, must affect his moral behaviour. The more 'sensitive' he is in this sense, the more he is likely to question the accepted moral standards of the people around him and to establish for himself standards that deviate in some degree from theirs. At the same time, his relative freedom from rationalisation makes him more likely than the 'resistive' man to live up to the standards he has adopted or to feel a keen sense of guilt when he lapses.

For schematic simplicity of discussion, it has been assumed that the moral interaction between individual people and their group, the nature and origin of their standards of behaviour, and the forces impelling them to obey a code or feel guilty, are all accessible to conscious inspection. We know, of course, that they are not. Psycho-analytic work (cf. Flugel, 1945) has shown some of the obscure mechanisms by which standards of conduct are established in the infant mind; it reveals how extensive are the unconscious and often foolish elements of the ideals by which we judge ourselves, and how unreasonably severe some people are in much of their self-condemnation. These are serious complications in any practical handling of an individual's moral attitudes, but not for an understanding of the basic relation between his nature as a social being and his evaluation of conduct.

5

THE GROUP'S ADEQUACY TO ITS MEMBERS

So much has been heard in psychology of the need for the individual to 'adjust' himself to his society that we may sometimes forget that social groups can in turn be assessed for their adequacy to their own members. 'Social adjustment' should be understood as a mutual interaction between group and individual. One of the pervasive pseudo-problems of psychology arises from the difficulty, in our structure of language and thought, of talking about a reciprocal process of this kind without phrasing it in terms of one side or the other. We are tempted, for instance, to say that the organism responds to environmental stimuli; only to meet the contrary assertion that environmental events would have no stimulus value but for the needs of the organism to which they relate; and though we may take refuge from this difficulty by emphasising that the organism and environment together constitute a field of forces we are not thereby provided with words and grammar that allow us to describe particular features of the interaction without starting from one side or the other. The individual's relation to his social environment provides one form of the general difficulty, and until we have mastered a new grammar for discussing interaction we must verbally misrepresent the process by making subject and object out of the equal interacting forces. To counteract the usual emphasis on the individual's adjustment to his group it may then be worth while phrasing the mutual relation in terms of the individual's requirements of his group.

A fully satisfactory social context for their activities includes for most people the opportunity of face-to-face contact with others whom they know and like, a recognised function in their group, and a sense of having the sanction of companions for a wide range of their individual values.

By their 'values' I mean, for psychological purposes, their desires and preferences, these, of course, being organised in systems, and to some extent hierarchies, of varying degrees of complexity and coherence in different people. In looking at one aspect of these systems of preference we can speak of 'interests', referring to the directions in which an individual is ready to be responsive, and all the discriminative ability, skills, information and other equipment that he has gathered in the course of exploring each of these directions of response. The possible modes of responsiveness are infinitely numerous, capable of being developed, as Woodworth (1918) suggests, from any potential interaction of organism and environment: if we can see, we may become interested in patterns of line, movement and colour; if we can hear, we may grow responsive to melody, harmony and rhythm; if we can value companions, we may develop social insight, affection and loyalty; if we can count, we may become mathematicians. From another aspect, our values consist in 'sentiments', organisations of dispositions towards this or that emotional attitude in the particular situations that we encounter when an interest is activated. We are not only capable of perceiving tunes but we like one and dislike another; the interest that we express by attending goes hand in hand with a sentiment that we express by either liking or disliking. The negative side of interests has to be included. A painter's highly developed discriminative response to colour means not only that some patterns of colour that other people ignore or dislike will appeal to him but that some patterns that they like, because of the rudimentary development of their values, will repel him.

Ordinary observations show the infinite variety of individual value systems that develop among members of a complex society. Without the opportunity given by the culture of a group, extraordinarily few human potentialities would be realised in any individual lifetime, as the condition of the 'wild children' suggests.

But once a good range of possible responses to the environment had been set going the child's developments of interest and sentiment may often carry him, in one direction or another, to preferences and points of view in which he cannot expect to enjoy the sympathetic understanding of the majority of those among whom —and through whose help as carriers of culture—his early development occurred. On the other hand, their services to him will have included that of putting him into touch with a great variety of subgroups organised around the specialised development of particular interests and systems of value; anything from aero-modelling to work in the mission field. His family and its friends will include members and former members of a large number of sub-groups, and his school, his church, his youth organisations and his reading matter will offer him contact with very many more.

In the development of the individual, the sub-groups that his community make available to him perform essential functions. They form the vehicles for various specialised aspects and features of the total culture, and as such they provide the opportunities by which he may realise part of his human potentialities. The discovery that there are bodies of people held together in some degree of companionship through their common interest in ornithology, swing music, church architecture, embroidery, drama, model railways or what not constitutes an invitation to explore this or that possibility of human experience. The social matrix out of which our effective interests develop has to be intimate and subtle. A recent inquiry (Campbell, 1952) among children whose progress in secondary school appreciably exceeded or fell below estimates of their ability (based on intelligence tests, scholastic progress in primary school and a general assessment by primary school teachers) shows the vital importance to the child's progress of the parent's values as expressed in the cultural level of the home and their attitude to education. Educational 'opportunity' is a complex matter; it is not equalised by providing schools suited to a child's capacity unless people to whom he has emotional ties give implicit 'sanction'— not mere verbal consent but some understanding and sympathy— to the developments of interest that the school invites. A social matrix of companionship and emotional rapport seems to be a necessary condition for most social development, and it is this that sub-groups provide.

Group psychology, especially when a large community is in question, is sub-group psychology. The term 'sub-group' can usefully include, not only organised groups with a defined structure, but even an ill-defined vague union of people who are aware of bonds of common interest and outlook holding them together at least loosely and for some purposes and occasions; it includes groups with less defined aims than those of what sociologists call 'associations', in which a fairly clear goal of action unites and organises people. Only a small proportion of pedestrians, for instance, belong to any association to secure their safety and convenience, but many more will feel from time to time some common concern with each other as a body of people contrasted with other road users. The two sexes and the various age levels in a community may also at times feel some common interest that unites them and is not shared with the community as a whole, and they are to this extent indentifiable sub-groups. The essential is some awareness of shared values. A collection of people identified by an external observer's criterion, such as that of belonging to the same blood-group, does not form a psychological 'group'; it would begin to do so only if its members took a pride in their blood-group or grew anxious about it, and also felt, however dimly, that they were sanctioned in their attitude by others with the same characteristic. Once a sub-group has formed it possesses not only some internal cohesion but also a set of relations, more or less defined and organised, with other sub-groups in the community.

The sub-groups of a complex society are innumerable, overlapping, indefinitely sub-divisible, and often unnoticed until some shift of attention makes us aware of what we had been overlooking. It may, for example, take an economic emergency to make us realise that in needing outsize clothes we have something in common with a certain number of our fellows who, given a spokesman, will begin to voice their grievances and bring pressure to bear on traders and government departments whose policy affects them.

Long after an individual has been initiated in the line of development represented by a sub-group his membership in it continues to be vitally important for his ease of mind. The further he goes along some specialised line of activity the less he can expect most members of the community to understand his work, grasp its worth or give discriminating appraisal of his achievement. For this kind of response he must turn to his specialised sub-group, whether it be his fellow-mathematicians who can recognise the beauty of a proof, the members of his photographic club, or his brothers in a religious order who have some understanding of his spiritual aims and difficulties. Sub-groups, in fact, make psychologically supportable a specialisation of human function and a remote development of interest that carry the individual well beyond the comprehension of most of his fellow-beings.

Not only interests, in the usual sense of the word, but the whole structure of an individual's values, from its main branches to its finest growing points, will be affected by the sub-groups of which he is a member. In particular, the features in which he is unique are largely an indirect outcome of the sub-groups to which he has access. For, as many writers have pointed out, the individual man's simultaneous membership of many sub-groups gives him freedom from the scale of values represented by any one of them and invites that independent comparison of one outlook with another which makes for uniquely individual points of view. There is no escape from the more compact, relatively undifferentiated community; its members conform or lose their only opportunity of social sanction. In more complex communities the availability of number-less sub-groups with diversities of value and outlook offers the individual some degree of freedom from the psychological pressure of his community as a whole. Only the ruthless use of centralised instruments of propaganda and governmental regimentation could take us back towards the conformities of life among the simpler primitive peoples.

The opportunities given by simultaneous membership in many sub-groups are in some respects dangers too. If we enjoy the sense of being sanctioned by other people when our activities conform with their values we should also admit the relevance of their criticism when we violate those values. It can easily happen that we evade relevant criticism by playing off one of our sub-groups against another; cheerfully English until we make some social *faux pas* we then recall that we are, after all, a bluff Yorkshireman and rightly contemptuous of these niceties, or caught unshaven at midday we feel more than usual solidarity with our bohemian friends who would laugh at such suburban embarrassment. The fact is that in a complex community we can find social sanction for almost any bit of our behaviour taken in isolation, and this means that responsibility for the total structure of our values falls more clearly upon each of us individually than it would seem to if we lived in a more compact community. (A suggestive study of some aspects of this topic is to be found in Riesman, 1950.)

Besides its actual members, judged as such by external criteria, a sub-group may have the loyalty of a large number of people who feel bound to it by similarities of aspiration and outlook. Sherif (1948) suggested the term 'reference groups' for the groups with which we ally ourselves by believing that we share their scale of values; as, for example, people who by upbringing or economic position are of one social class may ally themselves to what they believe to be the more congenial outlook of another. People's beliefs about the scale of values characteristic of various sub-groups in the community—both those they like and those they dislike— are probably of great importance in individual development; it is a matter on which much more psychological information would be useful. It is clear, at any rate, that a sub-group to which we ally ourselves without being recognised members of it, and from which we possibly draw great psychological support for our values, may be to some extent the creation of our own fantasy. For one thing, it need not consist of living people: it may well be made up of writers, artists, religious people or others whose works and way of life form part of our group's tradition, and to them we may turn for reassurance in holding to values that are slighted by most of our contemporaries. The pre-Raphaelites supported themselves not only with their contemporary brotherhood but also with the assurance of returning to a set of values that had been sustained by earlier painters. So, too, the Anglo-Catholics of the nineteenth century found support in the belief that their forms of worship and faith had the sanction of the early Church. A tremendously valuable part of the recorded tradition of a complex community consists in its thus providing social sanction and a sort of companionship for those living members of the group whose values can never expect wide contemporary support or, for one reason or another, have gone out of favour for the time being.

Obviously, too, this companionship with people we never meet has its dangers. It can be largely a creation of fantasy for confirming ourselves in an outlook that we should do better to change and one that perhaps never was sanctioned; if the figures of the past came to life they might promptly repudiate us. Like any golden age, these social groups created from the past may allow us too easily to ignore relevant criticism from living contemporaries. Our dependence on them may also, of course, be mainly an outcome of neurotic traits that prevent us from getting on with contemporary people who would be perfectly adequate to our less neurotic demands. It seems likely that fantasy companionship, familiar in children, is at all ages a fairly common outcome of the failure to find direct social satisfaction; a good many people have a freer flow of social feeling towards favourite broadcasters or film stars than they can allow themselves towards the people they know in real life. But the many possibilities of using imaginary companionship in a neurotic way do not alter the fact that social support from sub-groups formed of people long dead may be one of the most effective and valuable contributions of tradition to the living individual.

Besides the services they give the individual, sub-groups fulfil functions for the community as a whole. For one thing, they help the rest of us to assess the worth of individual achievement in specialised directions. Without the sub-group of mathematicians and physicists few of us would be able to feel certain that Einstein and Jeans were not charlatans, and even in matters nearer at home such as ballet, speedway riding, professional football or modern music, our judgements depend to a degree we cannot always estimate on the opinions of those we regard as expert. Like any other group, specialised sub-groups are also in danger of over-rigidity and unnecessary antagonism to new ideas, and therefore may fail for a long time to sanction individual advances which would be of value to the group itself. The experience of Lister among his fellow-surgeons is not unusual. At times it may happen that a stubbornly ill-judging sub-group yields in the end to pressure from the main community, a point that must be discussed in connection with the process of social innovation.

Again, from the standpoint of the community as a whole, sub-groups make possible what may be called a delegation of function, a sharing out of activities which cannot all be undertaken by each member of the group. Division of work and growth of special trades and professions is only one example of a wider process. F. C. Bartlett (1923) points out the importance in primitive societies of the growth of sub-groups to deal with certain impulses, especially that of fear, which would be disruptive of other activity if not kept well under control; he views such sub-groups as the wizards and priests as a means by which the community partially segregates impulses which might be a serious source of conflict and sees to it that any preoccupation with them shall be canalised within a small section of the community. In occupying itself with a special impulse or line of interest the sub-group is serving the main community and making available in special ways and on special occasions the results of its intensive cultivation of the interest. Nor need we confine these processes to primitive groups. In a modern society much the same process affects our attitude to doctors; we turn to them not merely for the physical effects of their knowledge and skill but also in order to shed upon them the load of anxiety about health, our own and our friends', which would otherwise be more disruptive than it is. We are relieved by their taking responsibility, even if it is the responsibility of saying that nothing can be done. In rather the same way a priesthood may be expected to adopt standards—for instance of honesty and meekness—which are given lip-service by the main community but would, in fact, conflict with many of its practices if they were adhered to scrupulously.

The importance of delegated functioning by sub-groups will be underrated if we suppose it limited to primitive impulses or the fundamentals of morality. It includes the development of interests and values which cannot be widely cultivated because most of us lack the necessary time and money and ability. The innumerable specialised activities, occupational or recreational, of a modern community have sprung from capacities and inclinations which we nearly all possess in at least rudimentary form and they therefore have a potential appeal to us. Without being able, or even very seriously wishing, to be farmers, secret service men, musicians, explorers, psychiatrists, miners or politicians, we are still in touch with these possible ways of life and aware of them as part of the potential richness of experience that our community has tapped. What we cannot do individually we can delegate to others of our group and, for instance, be glad, although we ourselves have no head for heights, that other people accept the challenge of Matterhorn and Everest and develop possibilities of human courage and skill in that direction. We are not immune from the appeal, though it may be largely excluded from consciousness, of the disreputable possibilities too; a good deal of popular journalism caters for the widespread interest of the community in activities that it leaves mainly to the disapproved sub-groups of the underworld, the dope pedlars, prostitutes, racing swindlers, jewel thieves, smugglers and so on.

Continuous changes occur in the degree to which a special interest or way of life is narrowly canalised within a small sub-group or given wider expression among the members of the community; economic conditions, shifts of moral outlook, and many subtler factors influencing the current fashions in this respect. Religious revivals illustrate the overflowing from time to time into wide areas of the community of preoccupations that at other times are the concern of comparatively small special groups. Bartlett (1923) suggests that social retrogressions may be understood in part as a sudden spread amongst a considerable part of the community of disowned tendencies that had been driven underground and maintained by small sub-groups. Occasional recrudescences in western countries of interest in witchcraft and the practices of magic may be of this kind. But the same process of ebb and flow between sub-groups and main community is constantly occurring in less dramatic and more important ways. For example the enjoyment of long country walks was a possibility of life that was maintained in England for years by a small and almost entirely unorganised group of people, and then, seemingly rather suddenly, spread so widely in the form of 'hiking' as to be a national craze. Between the wars, social workers commented on the relative decline in prostitution as a specialist occupation in favour of more widespread amateur promiscuity; here the balance between sub-group and general community is affected by broad changes of moral code. After the second German War the kind of dishonesty that was once fairly narrowly restricted to small groups of swindlers and thieves became widely current in the form of black marketing; and here economic conditions and governmental practices were contributory causes. But though some of the prominent causes can easily be seen, the intimate psychological processes involved in these broadenings and narrowings of the groups concerned with particular ways of life have not, as far as I know, been at all fully examined.

The richness of a culture and the interest of the lives led within it depend largely on its sub-groups and their specialist developments. In a fluently communicative society such as ours, with journalism, broadcasting and the ubiquitous fiction of novels, plays and films, it is easy to make imaginary contact with a vast variety of ways of life. It is this which, in amateur psychologising, is often disparaged as 'vicarious satisfaction'. While no one would deny the wastefulness of some kinds and degrees of participation through fantasy in the activities of other people it would be belittling one of the sources of richness in a complex culture to lump together all interest in the community's delegated functioning as a search for 'vicarious satisfaction'. Indeed, one of the necessary disciplines of life in a society such as ours is that of resting content at many points with this delegated functioning. Some of the discontent that many people feel arises from the fact that so communicative a society holds out an enormous number of apparent possibilities, most of which we are debarred from realising personally and directly because of the shortness of life and the limits of our energy and economic resources.

All this diversity of occupation, interest, ability, preference and outlook is held together as a more or less coherent whole in a community of interlocking and overlapping sub-groups. It is their availability and effectiveness which will largely decide whether the community is adequate to its individual members' needs. This point perhaps needs emphasis. An attractive and dangerous alternative

c

is to concentrate exclusively upon the sub-group's functions for the community as a whole and to pass from this to a view of the community as an organism with sub-groups subserving its functions, as the specialised structures of the body serve the biological organism. This is an ancient idea and constantly reappears, often rephrased in terms of whatever science or vocabulary happens to command deference for the time being. Its statement in *Coriolanus* has a brevity that more recent formulations lack.

> The Kingly-crowned head, the vigilant eye,
> The counsellor heart, the arm our soldier,
> Our steed the leg, the tongue our trumpter,
> With other muniments and petty helps
> In this our fabric. . . .

—these have rebelled against the greed of 'the cormorant belly' which, of course, answers the charge effectively, with the final moral for the mob:

> The senators of Rome are this good belly,
> And you the mutinous members.
>   (*Coriolanus*, I, i.)

The analogy between a social group and the living organism is at many points suggestive and useful. It serves dangerous political purposes in so far as it attributes the value of individual lives to the contribution they make as subordinate parts of a more important whole. If a social group lays claim to the integrity of an organism it implicitly assumes the right to restrict the functioning of the real organisms that make it up. It may be retorted that a social group must constantly claim this right, in the very fact of demanding obedience to laws. But those who make the laws are people, and it is a matter of crucial importance whether in the last resort they must as individual people justify to others what they do or whether they can switch the responsibility to a 'social organism' answerable to nobody. These problems take us into social philosophy and cannot be examined here. Psychologically, however, we can say that a man differs from any specialised structure of an organism in the wide range of potential functioning he possesses; although some of his activities may be more useful than others to his society they are not therefore more important to him. Moreover, unlike the specialised structures of a real organism, individual people may have a potential range of activity far beyond anything that their particular social group—the so-called 'social organism'—regards as humanly possible or is capable of using. Only in a limited sense does society create its individual members. In equally important senses they as individuals create the group; what is more, they each strive to shape it according to their own ideas, something that no specialised subordinate structure ever does to the organism of which it is a part.

The biological analogy, though it may lead to some useful insights, too easily sanctions the view that 'social adjustment' is only a matter of the individual's adjustment to his group. The group's adequacy to its members is an equally vital question. Many people in a society like ours are bound to feel that although in their simplest basic desires, material and social, they have the sympathy of most of the men and women around them, yet in much else that matters to them the social group in which they dwell is uncomprehending or hostile. If in some directions their individual development has been carried far there can be no certainty that the sub-groups concerned with nominally the same interests will in fact be able and willing to give them sympathy (cf. Chapter 12). Within limits this is no cause for lament. A necessary quality for the attainment of individuality is the ability to tolerate some degree of loneliness, in the sense of independent adherence to values that those around you will not support. At the same time, a group whose culture fails notably to elicit its individual members' possibilities of development or a group that handicaps its more highly developed members by extreme isolation must be judged inadequate to their needs.

Groups, in other words, may fail the members they produce. The examples of persecuted reformers, discoverers and other creative individuals comes first to mind, but among much more ordinary people the same thing is constantly occurring in a less dramatic form. There are schools that leave the less standardised children's dormant powers unawakened or crush back slightly deviant lines of interest when they show themselves, professions that grow too encrusted or bleak to make life tolerable for members who still have life in them, groups of neighbours who ridicule deviations from conventional behaviour and engrooved aspirations, and endless other groupings that fail more or less seriously to sanction (and to use effectively) a minority of their members. We can add at once that the odd man out often helps to create his social difficulties by defensive self-conceit and neurotic behaviour, and no one wants to advocate a society that devotes itself tenderly to the comfort of all its cranks. Yet the trend of too much social psychology and too much psychotherapy has been towards accepting the requirements of some social group as the standard towards which its members should necessarily aspire. This is one of the criticisms rightly made by Murphy *et al.* (1937) of the work of Moreno (1934) whose technique of studying group structure identified (amongst other things) the 'isolates' in small groups, and whose therapeutic efforts seemed always to be towards modifying the individual sufficiently to adapt him to effective membership of the group. The presence of relatively isolated members of groups may be a valid challenge to the group to enlarge itself or to limber up in some respect and adjust itself more effectively to some of its members. It *may* be; there is no rule.

6

DEPRIVATION OF SOCIAL SATISFACTIONS

Some degree of frustration of social desires (as of most desires) is an ordinary experience. It occurs in any of the three areas of need already mentioned: friendly contact with congenial people, sense of having a function in one's group, and knowledge of social sanction for one's scale of values. Homesickness in its simplest form is the most generally familiar experience of disturbance in that social framework of our lives that we normally take for granted. Fairly full psychological studies of the condition are available (cf. the summary by McCann, 1941), and it seems likely that although the conscious longing may be for familiar places and physical surroundings, the house, the village, the scenery and so on, these ultimately derive their value from association with the people to whom we are attached; the very word 'familiar' underlines the fact. One case is reported of a small boy who showed all the symptoms, physical included, of acute nostalgia when his parents went on holiday, leaving him at home in surroundings that were familiar but lacked the family.

Observations of herd animals early revealed the fact of their distress at separation from their fellows. Galton's account of the Damara oxen, and the eager return plunge into the thick of the herd made by the distressed animal that had been separated, is trite with repetition by the textbooks of psychology. Kohler's report (1925) on his apes is equally vivid:

'. . . the group connection of chimpanzees is a very real force, of sometimes astonishing degree. This can be clearly seen in any attempt to take one animal out of a group which is well established as a group. When such a thing has never happened before, or not for a long time, the first and only desire of the separated creature is to get back to his group. Very small animals are naturally extremely frightened, and show their fear to such a degree, that one simply has not the heart to keep them apart any longer. Bigger animals, who do not show signs of actual fear, cry and scream and rage against the walls of their room, and, if they see anything like a way back, they will risk their very lives to get back to the group.'

The occasions of nostalgia among human beings would be further evidence, if more were needed, of the inadequacy of a 'herd instinct' to explain human sociability, for it is notorious that almost unbearable homesickness may afflict people who are thickly surrounded by fellow human-beings, for instance in armies and boarding-schools. Clearly the presence of a herd, any herd, is not enough. Homesickness in modern armies has in fact been serious enough to attract the attention of military medical and welfare authorities in the American Civil War, the Franco-Prussian War, and both the great wars of this century. This nostalgia while in the thick of people is understandable as long as we remember that any tendency to sociability that may be natural to us is from the earliest days of infancy canalised into sentiments, especially into attachment to the mother and other members of the family. Growing up involves a gradual widening of the human circle to which we give a degree of liking and trust and from which we can derive social satisfaction. Great individual differences occur in the ease and success of this aspect of psychological weaning, and if insecurity keeps our social sentiments too sharply focused on a few people we are particularly likely to feel homesick on being separated from them. The persistence of a narrow canalisation of social impulse into sentiments formed around a few people is a form of social development that paradoxically produces *un*easiness in the herd.

Abrupt separation from their parents contributed to a wide range of neurotic disorders among children who were evacuated from areas exposed to German bombing in the last war (cf. Susan Isaacs, quoted by Edelston, 1943). Similarly, the experience of a period in hospital, especially for young children and those who have not been understandingly prepared for it, appears to involve great disturbance, often concealed, and may precipitate neurotic disorders in children predisposed towards them. This form of nostalgic disturbance was well described by Edelston (1943) who reported on many children whose behaviour disorders or psychoneurosis could be convincingly related to separation anxiety exacerbated by a time in hospital. Some of the older children among Edelston's patients described their homesickness or the fear that their mother was going to leave them. Many of the younger children showed the same anxiety in a resistance to talking about hospital at all: it might take the form of stubborn silence or flat denial ('I can't remember' or even 'I didn't go to hospital') or of subtler evasions such as sidetracking the subject by a studied interest in some toy or game. In general, Edelston's case studies suggested that the basic trouble with children whose experience of hospital contributed to neurotic disturbance was the sense of insecurity arising from the rupture of the relation with a loved person. At the same time he shows that, as one would expect, in most cases of serious or lasting disturbance, some over-dependence on the mother had already been evident before the period in hospital.

The relation of this kind of disturbance (which has been the subject of considerable inquiry by psychotherapists since Edelston wrote) to ordinary adult homesickness can be illustrated by an interesting transitional case of an adult with morbidly low tolerance for separation from his family. This was Henry James, Senior, father of the novelist. Burr (1934) writes:

'Henry James Senior gave his wife and children a devotion as touching as it was intense. . . . This sensitive affection made separation a tragedy. Alice James, in her Journal, gives a quaint picture of "Father's sudden return at the end of thirty-six hours—having left to be gone a fortnight—with Mother beside him holding his hand and we five children pressing close 'round him, as if he had just been saved from drowning and he pouring out as he alone could the agonies of desolation through which he had come".'

The desire for face-to-face companionship among those with whom we feel secure, and co-operation with them in the simpler concerns of life, usually remains strong even in people whose main interests are in subtler or more complex activities. The hermit, content in his communion with an unseen church, is a rare type. It is not unusual for people to experience some slight uneasiness at individual developments of value that take them away from their family and early associates; the weakening or rupture of some early sentiments which their new values imply is apt to produce regret or guilt. Their wish—or velleity—to get back to the simplicities of earlier companionship is seen in such customs as the return to the old home at Christmas, and the effort to recapture the spirit of family life in its happier aspects and even to re-enjoy the old games. The too frequent unreality of the occasion is powerless to eradicate the recurrent longing for what it symbolises. This kind of nostalgia with its strong undertow back to the sentiments of early life, is always likely to be tinged with regressive longings, unconscious or barely conscious, for the after-seeming ease of infancy with its apparently moderate demands and its rich rewards of affection.

Those whose work and ambition bring them for much of their time into competitive conflict with their fellows are naturally subject to a strong pull back towards simple fellowship and a social situation in which they can lose some of the insecurity that extreme competitiveness generates. Many find a semblance of that situation in sociable drinking, where the lulling and loosening effects of alcohol, strongly supported by conventions of *bonhomie* and mutual trust, give them a sense of being at one with the sort of people they have been trying to outsharp all day. Another expression of these regressive longings is found in the sentiments about 'home' and the 'old folk' that are always current in one or other of our popular songs. And sentiment is expressed in action by those successful business men who return at last to their native village to retire.

We can thus roughly indicate one kind of frustration in social desire as arising from some disturbance of the sentiments in which the broad need for companionship has been canalised. There is a likelihood that the longings then experienced will be tinged with, or readily pass over into, a more or less regressive wish for earlier or seemingly easier forms of social relation. Closely related to this form of frustration is the conflict that occurs when competitive aims produce constant antagonism between ourselves and other individuals or groups of people. Relief for the social malaise thus induced is sought in many everyday social activities associated with relaxation; and it seems probable that it is also found in the greater social cohesiveness and mutual trust which are produced by any great simplification of group outlook such as occurs when a nation is united by war or a major disaster or anxiety. This possibility has, of course, been stressed by the psycho-analytic account of war (which I have discussed elsewhere, 1941).

A rather different form of social deprivation comes about from having no adequate function in one's group, and no niche defined in terms of obligations to others and of reciprocal rights that they recognise. The impression that the group to which he nominally belongs is functioning perfectly well without him often contributes to the newcomer's initial discomforts in first going to work or entering the forces or any other well-patterned organisation in which his part in the pattern is not at first evident. It is, of course, most obviously in occupational terms that our social function is defined for most of us. The effects of being deprived of it were seen, as many social observers remarked, in the apathy and deterioration induced by long spells of unemployment in the nineteen-thirties, when it became clear that being idle because nobody wanted your work carried severe psychological penalties, apart from the economic. Something of the same kind appears as one form of the 'frustration' commonly complained of in large organisations such as government departments where it sometimes happens that people are kept busily occupied at work that seems to them to have no perceptible effect on anything the organisation does, or in which instructions are changed and countermanded so readily that the worker cannot believe he is contributing to any clearly conceived and steady policy. Basically, he feels that the work he can do is not taken seriously.

The same trouble is being given more attention nowadays as one of the difficulties of old age; the sense of having no effective function in the life of one's social group after retiring from employment is seen to be one of the psychological hazards that await us in later life. The solution of the problem implied by the work of some psychologists and others is the extension of the period of useful employment by a more careful analysis of the abilities that are still available in old age, so as to continue to a later age the economic and material usefulness associated with the middle period of life. Valuable as this may be for increasing the community's resources in manpower, it does not, of course, go far towards an analysis of the main problem. For it seems likely that the root of the difficulty lies in a deeply entrenched feature of western societies: the tremendously high value placed on the individual's contribution to the material prosperity of the group, in spite of the lip-service paid to other values, such as art, scholarship, religion, social wisdom, moral development. There is consequently a great over-emphasis on the middle period of life, the period of fertility in women and material productiveness in men. Childhood is viewed as a preliminary to this period and old age as at best an aftermath. This distribution of emphasis in looking at the life-span was greatly encouraged by the popular biology of the nineteenth century and its preoccupation with the physical survival of species. One of its results appeared in the strange view of play (derived from Groos's theory) as drawing its value from the fact of being a 'preparation for life'; as if play were not in itself a valid form of living activity but had to be justified by its serviceableness to something else. In reality, we feel quite differently about play. If, for instance, we could foresee that a child was doomed to die at the age of ten we should none the less accept the value of his playing fathers and mothers or Cowboys and Indians at the age of six. Psychologically—as distinct from biologically—living activity justifies itself by short-term standards, perhaps from moment to moment, in childhood certainly from hour to hour.

Since we know from experience that childhood justifies itself to the child without reference to middle life, so we can expect that old age could justify itself to the old, on its own terms. But a satisfactory social context for old age demands a group that takes seriously the values that one's life at that period can still effectively express. Such a group would really believe that a man is doing something of social importance if, for example, he meditates in solitude on the stages leading towards Nirvana, or reads *King Lear* with fresh understanding, or repeats on rare occasions some of the stories of tribal deities that he heard from old men when he was young. Moreover, the ageing man needs to have had encouragement to develop such values earlier in his life. Whatever they are, whether philosophy and music or bowls and gardening, they cannot be suddenly acquired. The dawning realisation of the need for some values that will outlast middle life has been one of the problems of middle-age to which Jung especially has given attention (cf. *Modern Man in Search of a Soul*, 1933). This problem of a threatened loss of social function in old age is, therefore, a problem of the community's scale of values. A community that deprives the old of a sense of still participating in serious social concerns is failing to sanction not merely the values of that age-group but a possible development of certain values, especially the less competitive and material, all through the life-span.

At this point, the convenient distinction breaks down between being aware of having a function in our group and being aware that the group sanctions our activities and the values they imply. Our activities, if they strike our fellow-beings as worth pursuing, *are* a function for our group: we are exploring possibilities of human experience that our companions are glad to see explored. If, on the other hand, what we do strikes them as incomprehensible or futile, so that any sub-group that might support us is ineffective, or so small that it feels its existence threatened, then the conditions are prepared for a subtler deprivation of social satisfaction, a nostalgia arising from lack of attunement with the dominant values of our group. It is not enough to be carrying out some simple, useful role in the community if at the same time the things we chiefly value are not given any understanding by others. We are then in the position of the castaway who has been received by a savage tribe and shares their simpler concerns for food, shelter and defence, but who can look to them for no sympathy with the chief developments of value that he brought with him.

In this area of social need, a kind of nostalgia occurs which is the penalty of creating and taking seriously a scale of values not compatible with the dominant scale of our period. It is true, of course, that if we make any individual exploration of experience we must tolerate some degree of this isolation; the question for a social group is whether it enforces an unnecessary and disabling degree of isolation on some of its potentially valuable members. In our society, the kind of experience that may then occur has fairly often been revealed by modern writers, much more often by them, of course, than by scientists, politicians, business men or others whose work keeps them nearer the central concerns of the community. The sense of living in a world of uncongenial values, and the relation of this experience to ordinary homesickness, are vividly conveyed in the account that J. M. Synge gave of *The Aran Islands* and the meaning they had for him. From time to time, he would escape from the uncongenial civilisation of London, Paris and Dublin, and take refuge among the Aran islanders, believing that he found in their simple culture something more in keeping with his own values. In fact, of course, though they did not jar on him in the same ways, they could give him little companionship in his more highly developed interests. He wanted to believe that their everyday concerns revealed indirectly a rather subtle culture, what he calls 'the real spirit of the island':

'Yet it is only in the intonation of a few sentences of some old fragment of melody that I catch the real spirit of the island, for in general the men sit together and talk with endless iteration of the tides and fish, and the price of kelp in Connemara.'

He had gone from one inadequate group to another. But the simpler culture still had a great appeal, and on one of his returns to the Irish mainland he expresses a bitter nostalgia for the islands:

'I have come out of an hotel full of tourists and commercial travellers, to stroll along the edge of Galway Bay, and look out in the direction of the islands. The sort of yearning I feel towards those lonely rocks is indescribably acute. This town that is usually so full of wild human interest, seems in my present mood a tawdry medley of all that is crudest in modern life. The nullity of the rich and the squalor of the poor give me the same pang of wondering disgust; yet the islands are fading already and I can hardly realize that the smell of the seaweed and the drone of the Atlantic are still moving round them.'

The half-expression he gives to his slight disappointment after living for some time with the islanders shows with beautiful clarity the unsuccessful search for adequate companionship in his interests and outlook:

'In some ways these men and women seem strangely far away from me. They have the same emotions that I have, and the animals have; yet I cannot talk to them when there is much to say, more than to the dog that whines beside me in a mountain fog. There is hardly an hour I am with them that I do not feel the shock of some inconceivable idea, and then again the shock of some vague emotion that is familiar to them and to me. On some days I feel this island as a perfect home and resting-place, on other days I feel that I am a waif among the people. I can feel more with them than they can with me, and while I wander among them they like me sometimes, and laugh at me sometimes, yet never know what I am doing.'

A predicament such as Synge's, it may be objected, is precisely what the existence of specialised sub-groups has been supposed to prevent. Why was he not satisfied with the companionship of the writers and artists whom he knew in London and Paris, backed, as they could feel themselves to be, by a rich cultural tradition? The question leads one to look more closely at the relation of sub-groups such as this to the main community. It seems as if a man like Synge (a later example is D. H. Lawrence, as I have tried to show in *A Note on Nostalgia*, 1934) is not content with membership of a sub-group that is much detached from the main concerns of a community. He evidently wanted to feel that a concern for the literary values that his writing expressed could grow out of the simpler concerns of a community for work, shelter, safety, rest, and the entertainment of stories and singing; he wanted his work (as his plays, of course, suggest) to be a refined development and specialisation of values that permeated the community, not the outcome of an alternative or alien scale of values.

Such a continuity between simple and complex values is perhaps possible when the sub-group occupied with advanced interests is fully respected and partly understood by the mass of the community. In our present society, the sanction given to advanced scientific work is of this kind; developed to a degree of extraordinary subtlety, often of quite uncertain utility, totally incomprehensible to most members of the group, it is yet given the sort of respect that leaves no doubt that its exponents are in the main stream of the community's life. In some ages, religious and spiritual developments of an equally remote kind and degree have been a true part of the value system of a community few of whose members could comprehend them. A relation of this kind between sub-group and community is very different from that of the fringe group of literary people, largely aware of defying the values of the main community, to whom alone Synge could turn in the hope of having his subtler values understood and supported.

This broad survey of nostalgia and related forms of social malaise suggests that a great range of human activity is likely to set up some degree of disturbance in the individual's social comfort. The process of growing up and taking part in the life of the adult group asks for a weakening of the early sentiments in which social responsiveness first found expression. The competitive struggle and pugnacity involved in a great deal of everyday work will in some measure thwart the wish for friendly companionship with others. One result is the activation of more or less regressive trends towards loosely sentimental or over-simplified forms of sociability.

The sense of having a function in the life of one's group is a further aspect of social need which in various circumstances may be denied. But besides wishing to contribute something at the simpler levels of the group's activity we also want to feel that our more highly developed interests and sentiments are attuned to the value system of our group, and that if we depend on a sub-group for detailed understanding of our concerns we can still feel that the main community willingly provides a niche for that sub-group. It seems clear that individuals need enough toughness and resilience to tolerate conditions that fall far short of complete social harmony; otherwise they would never develop any original lines of activity. But it remains true that at any given period in the history of a culture some people will be concerned with unfashionable, disparaged or uncomprehended values and will be subject to social deprivations not because they are 'socially maladjusted' in some morbid way but because their contemporary group is relatively insensitive to the range of values that means most of them. We are brought back to the fact that social groups are likely to fail a proportion of the members they produce and to make the psychological conditions of social life wastefully hard for many people whose work is eventually recognised as a valuable social possession

7

COMPETITION

All social experience is shot through with the contrast between the liking people feel for each other and the mutual antagonism that arises from clashes of attitude and aim when they pursue their own ends. The contrast begins in infancy with the ambivalence of the parents as a result of their dual role of cherishing and gratifying on the one hand and of restricting, denying and frustrating on the other. In later life we can to some extent distinguish the likable and the objectionable aspects of the people we know, and can then react with discrimination to the two. This introduces complexity into our relations, in place of the muddle implied by ambivalence in which one and the same undifferentiated object is both attractive and repellent. But even if fine discriminations, adequate to the complexity of the facts, have been achieved, there remains much tension in having to feel and behave very differently towards the same person at different times and in different aspects.

These contrasts of attitude, producing either confusion or complexity in those who experience them, appear in one of their clearest forms in the uneasiness we feel about competition in social life. Development as members of a human community involves learning to co-operate and at many points to yield; selfishness, greed and the refusal to share are treated as features of primitive unregeneracy that have to be subdued if the child is to grow into a passable adult. But in later childhood and adult life he finds that society is organised competitively and that now his job is to get the better of others. Social ideals and institutions concerned with co-operation and competition differ from group to group (for the outlook of some primitive groups, see Mead, ed. 1937), but in complex western societies the strongly competitive organisation of much adult life in economic matters, sport and games, courtship, and most other directions of social prestige, is notorious.

The first half of the twentieth century brought a revulsion among many serious thinkers from the whole idea of competition. It would not now be possible to go back to the outspoken competitiveness, uncomplicated by doubts, which characterised the nineteenth century in Britain. One sees it, for instance, as a thread running all through *The Diaries of Lady Charlotte Guest*, the aristocratic wife of the greatest iron-master of early Victorian Britain. Sometimes she expresses the anxiety she feels lest competitors should catch up (24th September, 1837), sometimes chagrin at disappointed competitiveness, as when her husband was made only a baronet (3rd July, 1838), sometimes relief at sucessful competition when the issue was in doubt (4th July, 1838), and sometimes a jubilant acceptance of competition as a main feature of her life, as in the entry for 27th April, 1839:

'I went for the first time to see the new Office in the City, 42, Lothbury, it is well situated and very commodious. They have paid me the compliment of fitting up a room for me there, and I think it is a retreat that I shall often be tempted to resort to from the gaieties and interruptions of Grosvenor Square. I have so schooled myself into habits of business that it is now more congenial to me to calculate the advantage of half per cent commission on a cargo of iron than to go to the finest Ball in the world. But whatever I undertake I must reach an eminence in. I cannot endure anything in a second grade. I am happy to see we are at the head of the iron trade. Otherwise I would not take pride in my house in the City and my Works at Dowlais, and glory (playfully) in being (in some sort) a tradeswoman. Then again, my blood is of the noblest and most princely in the Kingdom, and if I go into Society, it must be the very best and first. I can brook no other. If I occupy myself in writing, my book must be splendidly got up and must be, as far at least as decoration and typography are concerned, at the head of literature. . . .'

Lady Charlotte intended this Diary to be read (cf. 12th November,

1837), and there is evidence of her being an intelligent, kind and civilised woman. Her unashamed avowal of the wish to outdistance others as one of her main motives is something that would hardly have been possible a century later, and it serves as a useful datum line for assessing the change.

For the other extreme, of societies in which competition is kept at a minimum, we have instances from anthropological reports on primitive peoples. One of the best known is that of the Hopi Indians of Arizona, among whom the singling out of anyone for special praise or responsibility arouses uneasiness from childhood onwards. Comparison between children's work in school is avoided by teachers because it produces only resentment, not emulation. Men are reluctant to accept jobs as foremen in government-sponsored undertakings on the reservation; if they take them they are accused of thinking themselves better than others and are badgered by disparaging remarks. They avoid comparing the value of one another's work; 'a highly skilled stone-cutter is perfectly content to accept the same wages as an unskilled day labourer' (Thompson, 1950). The whole picture suggests a culturally induced reaction-formation against competitive trends that might otherwise induce anxiety.

A specifically economic institution that minimises the effects of competition is seen in the Fijian 'keri-keri', a form of sanctioned cadging. By this, a man who is in want of some material possession can ask for it from any kinsman who has more than enough for his immediate use. The request has to be granted; the commodity is not a loan, for it is not returned, nor a gift, for it is demanded by right. It carries only the reciprocal obligation to allow similar 'cadging' if at any time the recipient has more of some property than the donor. It naturally produces tension when European influences begin to take effect, for such practices as thrift, saving up commodities for future use and accumulating stock for trading purposes are put out of the question.

Competition among their members is evidently a problem that diverse societies and periods have handled in widely different ways, and the part that it shall be allowed to play in the affairs of our own society is still a matter for political controversy. While some writers (e.g. Reavely and Winnington, 1947) treat it as almost entirely an evil to be eliminated, others think of it as a necessary spur to effort and speak of the 'incentive of competition'. Psychological discussion is justified in trying to clarify the nature of the process about which such conflicting sentiments are held.

It seems advisable to distinguish first between friendly competition and serious. In the first, most familiar in games, the competitors are co-operating to provide both a means of testing their skill or prowess and an intrinsically enjoyable game; the loser may be disappointed that his skill was not greater, but his main purpose will have been achieved in having had it exercised and enjoying the game. This is true of the ideal game and the ideal loser; in reality, contamination with serious competition frequently occurs. In 'serious' competition both people want something in short supply, or in shorter supply than can satisfy what they take to be their needs, needs for instance of material goods, money, prestige, affection, security. Such competition may be subject to control by sentiments and social institutions that mitigate its rigour, but it remains serious in that the success of one competitor means that the other is deprived of what he hoped to gain when he embarked on the competition.

However much they fuse in practice, these two forms of competition are distinct on account of the relation between the competitive effort and social sentiments: in friendly competition, social impulses and the wish to excel have a final common path and reinforce each other; in serious competition, if one's liking for the competitor, one's consideration for him as a human companion, were allowed much development, it would conflict with vigorous pursuit of the activity that brings him loss. In serious competition, consequently, there is conflict within the competitor to the extent to which he is socially responsive; if he is capable of social impulses they must in some degree be checked, whether by repression or by conscious inhibition. This conflict within the competitor is the central problem in serious competition; it provides the ground for opposed views on the desirable role of competition in social life.

No psychological support is available for the idea that competition is a motive force in its own right. We always compete for something we desire—money, power or what not—and the motive force is the desire; competition, the effort to do better than others in the same scramble, is simply the attempt to overcome an obstacle to the desire. When we speak of competition as an incentive—when teachers give children the spur of competing for positions in class, for instance—we refer to an extra effort which is made in order to secure some further satisfaction than the completion of the task would give by itself. The competition is *for* something. When we say that we have a motive to excel others, almost regardless of the matter in which we excel, we mean that we have a wish for their esteem, and that in our culture we can gain that by outdoing them at this, that or the other. In Hopi culture, the same desire for esteem leads people not to outdo one another, and there, where competitive success does not bring social esteem, the so-called 'motive to excel' is missing. It seems best, therefore, to regard the striving to excel others as instrumental in satisfying some other motive, not as giving a direct satisfaction in its own right. The motive is the desire for what successful competition brings, not the desire to compete.

It is true that competition often looks as if it were a driving force. We constantly see men whose reasonable needs for goods in short supply (especially money, power and deference) must long ago have been met but who go on competing for them, apparently for the sake of competing. Two possible explanations present themselves. One is that the work involved in these people's competitive activity—business or politics, for instance—offers many satisfactions in addition to the winning of money and power. It may, for one thing, give opportunities of benevolence. For another, probably more important, it makes possible the continued use of technical skills and knowledge, astute judgement and social ability which have been gathered in a life-time of such work and the exercise of which has become a satisfaction in its own right ('functionally autonomous' as Allport (1938) puts it). The second explanation, the main one in some cases and probably relevant in some degree to all, is that competitiveness is frequently compulsive and gives its chief satisfaction for reasons of which the competitor is unconscious or very imperfectly aware.

Neurotic competitiveness forms a fairly familiar pattern that may run through the whole texture of a personality. One sees it in the conversationalists who talk not in order to exchange views but to display their cleverness, the business men who are gratified at getting the better of one another, no matter what for, the men in professional life who put careerism before the standards proper to their work. In its more emphatic forms, this kind of life is a flagrant neurotic manifestation, no doubt often beginning in early sibling jealousy or similar sorts of insecurity; seeing marks of affection and respect being given to others sets up anxiety lest there may not be enough to go round. This poor toleration of others' success makes the victim uneasy about his own condition even when he had previously been satisfied, and it results in his always trying to cap the achievement of others regardless of his direct satisfaction from the achievement it leads him to undertake. This is the nearest we come to finding competition a driving force—when competitiveness has become a personality trait. Even then it can safely be taken to have originated in the need for something else.

In a less extreme form, competitiveness of this kind is notoriously common as one irrational strand amongst the many strands of motive and incentive. It was clearly very prominent in nineteenth-century England, rationalised by the ruthless economic threats of that age, and it is from the outcome of this personality trait of competitiveness that the twentieth century's revulsion reasonably occurred.

Yet to regard competition as nothing but an evil, to be minimised at any cost, is an extreme view of which the implications are not always seen. It has in the past received support from the belief that there exists enough of every sort of good, material and psychological, to satisfy everyone's reasonable wishes. Popularisers of economic doctrines between the wars spread the impression that there was enough of everything for everyone in a fabulously prosperous world if only we improved our distribution methods or currency practices or political intentions; but it looks as if this was a fantasy. It looks as if for many years we shall live in societies where material goods and services will be in too short supply to satisfy everyone's expanding wishes. In such a situation a policy of equal shares for everyone regardless of relative ability and effort would bring about a more extensive alteration in our institutions, especially those concerned with incentives to work, than most people would favour. That a very low level of competition can be established in human societies, and culturally stabilised, the anthropological evidence puts beyond doubt; but it is not clear that this can be achieved without sacrifice of other things that 'advanced' peoples have thought desirable, among them a high level of material prosperity and the possibilities (for instance, of health, long life, education) that go with it. What degree and what forms of competition are to be incorporated in a social system are questions to which each group gradually gives an answer in its institutions and customary outlook; and the answers to those questions affect many other aspects of the group's life.

Competition for such psychological gratifications as social esteem and distinction needs to be examined more closely. It is a case where the cart is rather often put before the horse. It makes good sense to value social esteem if it means that, knowing you and knowing your achievement, the people whom you respect think well of you and what you have done. But here, as often in social life, two desires and loyalties may conflict. Part of our development has consisted, especially in early life, in securing the affection and regard of other people by learning to do what they approve of; but another part consists in discovering for ourselves the worth of some interests, attitudes and achievements and helping to make a social world in which others also recognise those values. If we tip the balance too far to the latter side we run into the danger of arrogant self-satisfaction and disregard for relevant criticism. If we tip it the other way, we find ourselves running after esteem by submitting slavishly to the standards set by others and exerting ourselves to do things that have little direct value for us but are merely instrumental in gaining the esteem of others; a programme that only amounts to keeping up with the Joneses. It involves not only the 'conspicuous consumption' that Veblen (1899) analysed but often an equally futile conspicuous production (whether of flower-beds or scientific articles), a conspicuous attendance at cultured parties, a conspicuous membership of committees and conferences.

Moreover, once we take the winning of esteem as an end to be directly sought, and not just a fortunate by-product of having done good work within an adequate social group, we open the door to every technique of self-advertisement and careerism. Those who engage in such practices have put the cart before the horse with a vengeance: they want to be assured by others that they and their achievements are valuable, but they get esteem for what they half-know to be spurious achievement. The result is often an insatiable appetite for more prestige and the reassurance it gives, an appetite characteristic of the compulsive careerists in every occupation.

In its less neurotic forms, competition for social prestige need be no more socially disruptive than the friendly competition of games, where the satisfaction lies in having successfully measured yourself against a relevant standard of achievement. It betokens a high measure of social good fortune if a man has a group or sub-group whose range of understanding and values provides a relevant criterion for his best achievement.

8

SOCIAL STATUS

Competition for social esteem and distinction presents a number of special problems. It involves questions of social 'class' and stratification and of occupational prestige, and it has for long been a tangled topic in social psychology. Here it may be best to approach it not by any attempt to define 'class' but in a more piece-meal fashion by noting a large variety of factors which make for esteem in our society, but which are not closely correlated with one another and may contribute in very different degrees to the total esteem that an individual excites in those around him.

To begin with, we can note the standing that a man or woman occupies in the limited sphere of an occupational sub-group, whether he is a skilled tradesman or a labourer, a Q.C. or a junior counsel, a canon or an archdeacon, whether she is a sales-girl or a buyer, an assistant teacher or a head mistress, a staff nurse or a ward sister. At its most obvious, a worker's standing in his occupation is indicated by clearly defined ranks, as in the fighting services or the police force; but very much subtler and more spontaneous classifications occur in large organisations such as industrial firms, and Elton Mayo (1933) describes the importance to the social relations among workers at the Hawthorne Works of the Western Electric Company of groupings based upon rather fine differences in the skill required for various types of work. He underlines by more systematic observation the kind of thing that was noted more journalistically by Whiting Williams (quoted in Moore and Hartmann, 1931) who worked as a labourer in a steel factory; after accepting without much enthusiasm promotion to the mill-wright's gang, with a very small increase in pay, he was astonished to discover what a distance he had covered socially and how enviable his new job seemed to his former mates, to such an extent, he says, that had his wife been living in the neighbourhood she would have been watched closely by the labourers' wives to see if she were still willing to associate with them. This may be an extreme case, possibly an exaggerated account, but it emphasises an undoubted reality of stratification within an industrial concern.

It is becoming a familiar fact that many industrial disputes about wages are the outcome of constant scrutiny to ensure that wage differences reflect differences of status based on skill, responsibility, seniority, and sometimes more conventional values. During the war of 1939–45, for instance, problems of this kind occurred frequently: skilled maintenance fitters were disgruntled because women running the machines might earn by piece-work more than the fitters who kept the machines capable of being run; adolescents could sometimes earn as much as adults, and women as much as men; and fathers might find their daughters bringing home higher wages than their own. In an excellent study of the psychological significance of women's wages in two war-time engineering factories, Davis (1944) gives the example of operators, paid by bonus system, and examiners, paid by time rate, working side by side:

'The difference in the amount of payment, since the operator frequently earned more than the examiner, sometimes led to jealousy and bad feeling; the examiners tended to form a social group of their own, from which their working companions, the operators, were excluded.'

As far as these distinctions of standing within an occupation are appreciated by the public they contribute to the individual's esteem in the community as a whole; the production manager of a small factory will probably be given higher status than a solicitor's clerk, though not higher than a solicitor's. The individual's supposed degree of independence and initiative and the number of people working under his direction are important factors in this context.

However, a man's status in the community at large will not closely parallel the status he has within his occupation. A junior position in one occupation may give higher general standing than seniority in another. There are clearly other factors which affect our standing in the community as a whole, some of them more decisively.

To begin with, 'birth' still counts. Being born into a family that already enjoys respect, for whatever reason, is an initial advantage; it may secure some deference for a person who has few or none of the other attributes that win esteem, and it may in all sorts of ways, direct and indirect, facilitate the attainment of some of those other attributes. 'Birth' in this sense counts for something at all economic levels and at all points of the obsolescent social scale that used to run from king to serf. The children of a highly esteemed foreman have in this respect an initial advantage over the children of a labourer, one that may be of great practical import-ance, for instance, in getting their first job. Sound reasons may guide us, other things being equal, in being initially prepared to give esteem for the sake of social connexions conferred by birth, but sound reasons only too easily—and again at all economic levels —shade over into deference from motives of snobbery and into the numberless forms of nepotism and favour-currying. It goes without saying that in our culture 'birth' matters much less than it used, largely because practical privileges affecting children's material welfare and educational opportunities are no longer associated with it as closely as they once were.

Another, and immensely important, gradient of respect in our culture is provided by money and purchasing power (including the purchasing power delegated to members of firms). Even fairly poor shoppers put themselves for the moment into a position of superiority when they consider a purchase (except of goods in very short supply); the policy indicated by the slogan 'the customer is always right' is (at least when there are more goods than customers) a recognition that people are glad to pay for a slight show of deference as well as material goods. The fact that the possession of money, and nowadays of an expenses account, can so readily be indicated by clothes, houses, cars, travel and so on leads, of course, to vast expenditure of the kind that Veblen called 'conspicuous consumption', expenditure that serves to establish one's position on the gradient of respect created by money.

Education provides a further gradient. Its significance is complex. At one time, the opportunity for extended education was so closely associated with privileges of birth or wealth that it gained a factitious esteem on that account. But besides this it stood for intrinsic values that were widely current, so that even the 'poor scholar' was a respected figure; and to some extent this latter value is still effective, especially through its association with the contemporary prestige of science. Moreover, as the opportunities for education have gradually come more into line with the capacity to use them, the fact of having had a lengthy education is increasingly taken to testify to one's general ability, and in fact it is sometimes supposed (to the ultimate embarrassment of universities) that an extended academic education is necessary or proper for anyone of good ability, regardless of the type of interest development in which his ability is expressed. Futhermore, to add to the confusion, long education is often associated with the training necessary for entering occupations of high standing. The outcome of this tangle of ideas, however, is the clear fact that among the attributes making for social esteem is that of having had a lengthy education and, to some extent, of revealing the qualities of mind which it is supposed to foster.

Although the mere possession of money, regardless of how or whether it is earned, is one claim to esteem, the nature of the occupation that yields the money constitutes another gradient of respect in the community as a whole, and nowadays probably the most important gradient of all. To understand the factors that define an individual's standing in his community, therefore, we have to consider what factors affect the prestige of his occupational sub-group. Here again it seems advisable to work piecemeal, identifying various gradients of respect, and also noting in advance that an occupation with a high position on one gradient may have a lower position on others. To begin with, of course, the general values of a given culture will affect the prestige of occupations in so far as they are associated with some recognised value: the warriors in one group will be given very high respect, the priests in another, the politicians in another; so, too, in one group (or in one of its phases) the prostitutes will be selected for specially low regard, in another the usurers, in another the shop-keepers, in another the kulaks. Apart from this, however, one or two fairly general principles governing the prestige of occupations in our society can be detected.

The supposed rareness of the qualities needed for an occupation plays a rather important part in its prestige. It may reasonably be held that the social function of bakers is by no means less important than that of doctors, but bakers have less prestige because, for one thing, we believe that people capable of learning how to bake are more easily found than potential doctors.

Associated with this last reason for respecting an occupation there often goes the length of training it requires, and nowadays this has come more and more widely to be associated with the extent of general education that precedes occupational training. A long preparation for a job, whether in the form of general education, professional training, or a period of low earning before a practice could be established, meant in the past the possession of money, and derived further prestige value from that fact. But it seems likely that even if the public eventually comes to provide the money for everybody's occupational training there will still be a tendency to esteem the jobs needing the long training and the trainees on whom it is thought to be worth while spending so much money. To have its full prestige value the long training must precede paid occupation in the work, no doubt because this heightens the value of the learner on whom it is thought to be worth while spending money. The result is likely to be an expensive proliferation of training courses where apprenticeship would be better. Many nurses in England have thought that the social standing of their profession would be higher if they had 'student status' instead of being employed during the long period of their training, and this view, whether sound or not, illustrates the fact that length of training is widely held to earn respect for an occupation.

A further very important factor is the extent of the individual responsibility assumed by the member of an occupation. If we find that the carpenter or even the butcher is incompetent we can make a change without much harm having been done; but if the surgeon blunders the effects may be more serious. (Cf. Elliott Jaques, 1956, for a suggestive and partly convincing attempt to define 'responsibility'.) The community tends—other things being equal—to give most respect to the occupations whose members have been entrusted with most individual responsibility.

In some ways allied with this point is the extent of independent initiative and freedom from the commands of a superior that the member of an occupation is credited with. The privilege of doing one's job without being under orders gains high general esteem; so too, conversely, does the fact of having others under one's orders. This undoubtedly forms one of the attractions of being in business for oneself, even in a small way.

It must be repeated that these (and no doubt many other) gradients of respect which affect the status of occupations crisscross in all directions. The qualities needed for being a film-actor may be rarer than those for being a doctor, and the training may be as lengthy; on these gradients of respect the film-actor stands high. But doctors have a higher standing on the gradients of education, individual responsibility and the value of their functions. If, therefore, we make a judgement about the relative social prestige of film-actors and doctors it will represent some rough averaging of their position on these and several other gradients, each weighted according to the importance it seems to have for us at the moment. Industrial and agricultural work is of no less importance to the community than clerical work, often better paid and giving the worker more initiative, but the 'white-collar' job still has more prestige in many sections of society, not merely on account of its cleanliness, but also partly because it has been taken to imply better education, with all that that confusedly implies in turn.

The money rewards offered by the various occupations are of psychological as distinct from economic significance in two contrasting ways. In the first place income (from whatever occupation it comes) contributes directly to social status, and does something to make up for deficiences on other gradients of respect. But in the second place the money paid for work is an indication of the value attaching to the work in the eyes of the community; it is an index of the prestige accorded to the job for other reasons. This latter meaning of wages and salaries (as distinct from mere income of unspecified source) has important social implications. Long-continued low wages in an industry are felt to be a psychological disparagement as well as an economic hardship, and when this implied estimate of the worth of an occupation is much at variance with its real importance, as it was for years in coal-mining, formidable difficulties eventually result, both in recruitment and from the attitude to the community of the disparaged sub-group. Nursing is another occupation in which salaries have been felt by many to indicate too low an estimate of the worth of the job; here it was partly the importance of actual money as a convenient index of esteem that resulted eventually in the conversion of emoluments into nominal salary (from which the value of the emoluments was then deducted). A further result of the psychological meaning of wages and salary is the constant pressure of each occupational sub-group to maintain in terms of money a position relative to other occupations which corresponds with its worth as judged by other criteria. Thus while the police press for higher wages the firemen press for parity with the police. Bartlett (1923) has drawn attention to the constant effort of sub-groups to extend their power in the community, and the concern of occupational sub-groups with their members' earnings is, apart from its economic significance, one aspect of this psychological tendency.

The factors affecting social esteem which have so far been noted are obviously related to the broad grouping of people into social 'classes'. Birth, money, education and occupation have been associated with each other in the past and to some extent still are. To the extent that they go together they encourage the labelling of people in terms of class, with all its associated stereotypes, although the class structure that established the concept has largely disintegrated. There is no doubt that it still has importance in social life, and affects such matters as marriage and the choice of friends. Constellations of interest, taste, ambition, recreation and so forth are closely enough associated with 'class' to make it a useful means of labelling people for the practical purposes of market research. Class membership is now largely what an individual achieves, rather than what he was born to, although early influences may prevent full subjective assimilation to the class into which, by the standards of money, education and occupation, he has risen or sunk.

The fact that these gradients of respect form a fairly well-organised constellation becomes clearer if we notice other gradients that are not part of the same constellation. High achievement in athletic sports may be quite independent of it, so may religious devoutness, personal beauty, and the possession of valuable moral qualities and traits of character such as courage and good sense. We no longer expect to find these things closely associated with any 'class', nor does our recognition of them in an individual affect the way we would assess his 'class' if we were obliged to do so—for instance, in interviewing for a market survey. Two other gradients of esteem and deference in our social group, sex and age, both of them working in complicated and contradictory ways, are also outside the cluster of variables that make up the vague concept of class.

Up to this point, no reference has been made to the various external signs by which, in the absence of closer knowledge, we may guess at a person's 'class', among them things like speech, clothes and table-manners. It seems vital here to distinguish between two types of these signs: on the one hand those points of behaviour that are important almost exclusively as supposed signs of class status, and on the other those that may indicate class affiliation but also seem of value in themselves and therefore contribute directly to our regard for the person who has them. Among the first kind are the more arbitrary matters of speech accent and idiom (e.g. 'Pardon?' and 'dinner', 'lunch' or 'luncheon') and the table-manners required for the more elaborately formal meals; these signs of status may also change arbitrarily, as for example in the first German War when at one period it was officers who smoked pipes and other ranks cigarettes and at another vice versa. On the whole, such arbitrary signs of class affiliation now count for much less than they once did, for to value them we must retain (whether consciously and avowedly or not) some respect for the more obsolescent notion of classes defined mainly by birth and early associates. Yet of course they still matter enough, in a society as class-conscious as ours, to be the object of an immense volume of effort and anxiety by mothers bringing up children and by many young people themselves. In 'lower class' and 'lower middle class' families who aim at higher class status than the occupational and financial position of the father would confer, the arbitrary indices of class affiliation are often of painfully great importance.

The second kind of status indicator is to be found in matters of habit and customary behaviour which, besides being associated with various strata of wealth, education and occupation, are valued in themselves. They include some of the simpler ceremonials of eating, such as the use of a fork instead of fingers and the provision of clean plates and cutlery. They include various habits of personal hygiene, from the frequency and extent of washing to putting your hand up when you cough. And they also include customary modes of speaking that go beyond matters of accent and idiom: such things as the techniques of verbal phrase, intonation, mode and frequency of interruption, and accompanying facial expression that allow differences of opinion to be discussed without creating an atmosphere of dispute. Among English psychologists, Pear (1938, 1955) has for long given special attention to signs of class status in our culture. And, in spite of the differences in American culture, class distinctions are clearly enough visible there to have been studied in great detail by American psychologists (cf. Warner and Lunt, 1941, Havighurst and Taba, 1949, West, 1945).

Most English people nowadays agree that the old forms of class distinction are rightly obsolescent and that the more rapidly they decay the better. Our embarrassment about their continued existence is evident in the partial taboo on references to class that many psychologists have remarked on; class differences are referred to apologetically, if at all, by most middle-class people. We have reacted in this way against the gross injustices and social waste that used to occur, and in a less degree still do occur, because of the needless inequality of opportunity that goes with birth into one social stratum rather than another. But it seems open to question whether even the total decay of the old system will obliterate distinctions between groups of people based on clusters of differences in their outlook and behaviour. At the present time, differences of this kind divide people who, by the rough and ready criteria of the social investigator, all belong to the same 'class'. Thus in Mass Obser-

vation's study (1943) of a small war-time works it is reported that
the girls in the machine shop were looked down on by what the
report calls 'C-class girls from other departments' as rough and un-
mannerly, 'a very low class of girls'. Many of the machine shop
girls resented this and were, in return, hostile to those who looked
down on them. A few, however, though equally 'C-class', felt it
themselves and kept aloof from the girls around them, saying such
things as: 'They're very mixed. You'll see. This is the worst place
to come to. I don't like it at all. I don't mix with any of them.'
This kind of thing is familiar to any industrial psychologist, especially
if he has worked in small factories, for the reputation of the 'class
of girl' who is to be found in a particular factory affects recruitment
and consequently tends to be self-perpetuating. The social judgement involved here is obviously different from simple class snobbery
of the old sort.

It is based ultimately on a set of perfectly direct preferences. If
you don't like swearing (or like only a limited vocabulary of swear-
words), if you would rather speak quietly than shout, if you
object to abusive quarrelsomeness, if you have views as to what is a
dignified relation with the foreman, if you would rather go to the
pictures than to a wrestling match, and so on, then you find yourself 'not mixing' with some groups of working companions. How
ever 'classless' a society may become, birds of a feather are likely to
go on flocking together. Groups united by particular interests, and
groups united by broad similarities in standards of behaviour, will
continue to form and perpetuate themselves.

This tendency admittedly holds psychological dangers which
lead back towards the prejudices of the older class system. Notably
there is the danger of supposing the members of any group to be
much more similar to each other than they really are and consequently of labelling individuals in terms of stereotypes, a process
that creates misunderstanding, inflicts injustices on many people,
and prevents us from recognising and benefiting from the real
individual qualities that count. The reaction against class distinctions,
like the reaction against 'racial' and national distinctions, is
part of a broader movement towards seeing and assessing people
as individuals, without preconceptions and bias set up by their

D

group membership. But this healthy movement is not in the long run aided by a sentimental refusal to notice group differences, nor by a well-meant denial that after contact with different groups we find ourselves preferring the majority of the members of one to the majority of the members of another. We have seen the decline —though by no means yet the extinction—of a social order in which membership of classes was established almost exclusively by birth. In its place it seems likely that we are getting not a classless society but a society in which broad levels of esteem still exist, related in part but not exclusively to the prestige of occupations, and in which the attainment of any given level depends more upon what the individual does than upon what his family did before him.

9

LEADERSHIP

The topics of competition and social status can scarcely be left without some discussion of leadership, a social process associated with them although in anything but a simple way. For instance, positions of leadership give esteem and high status, but high status of various kinds may be possessed without leadership, and recent trends in democratic countries have been towards preventing unearned social status from counting as much as it once did in securing positions of leadership. Again, competition affects the emergence of leaders, but the highly competitive man or woman is most unlikely to be an effective leader.

The record of social psychology in handling the topic of leadership is not gratifying. For a science it has too much moved or not moved with the times, reflecting current views and expressing them in slightly unfamiliar terms. The abstract analysis of 'authority' by political scientists and sociologists has not provided much that psychology could assimilate, and on the whole its treatment of leadership has been tethered more closely to the needs of practical affairs. This is in many ways an advantage, but basic psychological analysis has not in the main gone far at any time beyond the terms in which practical needs for leadership were framed by the more enlightened sections of ordinary non-technical opinion.

Thirty or forty years ago, the notion of leadership went with *esprit de corps* as part of the mental stock-in-trade of schoolmasters and captains of industry. Psychology followed in their footsteps, burrowing a little and emerging with a fact or two about the intelligence quotient of schoolboy leaders in relation to the average of their group, and a few platitudes about decisiveness, initiative and so forth (nobody being clear whether these were different unitary traits of personality, different aspects of one trait or bundles of separate habits). This phase was soon modified through the recognition by sociologists and psychologists—not, one would think, going far beyond ordinary good sense in this respect—that there are many varieties of leadership. Common observation and reflection then produced ways of classifying leaders according to categories that varied only a little from one scheme to another. That suggested by F. C. Bartlett (1926) was as good as any. He distinguished the institutional, the dominant and the persuasive types of leader; the institutional deriving his prestige and authority very largely from an established office in the group with institutions and customs for its support, the dominant depending to a great extent on self-assertion and decisiveness and the persuasive drawing his power from an ability to sense rapidly what his group is thinking and feeling and being able to formulate for them what they are ready to think and feel next.

Connected with this kind of approach was a recognition that the nature of the group, its circumstances and the kind of task it was facing all helped to decide what type of leader would emerge at a given time and what changes in leadership might be expected as the situation altered. The change in Britain from a peace-time to a war-time Prime Minister is a familiar example; the effective leadership of the native porters on one of the Everest expeditions is reported to have changed from one man to another when the climbing began to be hard; and everyday instances of the same thing in industry, business and public life are easily observed in spite of the tendency for the rigidity of institutional leadership to obscure them. This recognition of the group's situation and task as decisive factors in the emergence of one leader or another makes it clear that in any complex group there may be a multiplicity of diverse roles into all of which some kind and degree of leadership can enter. The House of Commons provides a ready example: the Speaker, the Prime Minister, the Leader of the Opposition, the Leader of the House, the party whips, chairmen of committees, leaders of rebel groups within parties, all exercise a different kind of leadership which is created at least in part by the needs of the group they are leading.

Where the older view tended to see the potential leader imposing himself on the group or competing for leadership, the recent tendency has been for psychologists, partly under the influence of Lewin (1948), to see the group gradually (and in the main wordlessly) defining its needs and interests, outlining roles to be filled and finding one or other of its members emerging to fill them (cf. Cartwright and Zander, 1960). These processes involve continuous interection between individuals and the group as a whole: awareness of a group's need may come only because the beginning of a role is perceived, and the role may appear to be created only because somebody has started to fill it. It is presumably in some such way as this that the regular reappearance of stock roles in similar groups is to be understood. Committees, for instance, frequently produce a provocative and aggressive member, another who is tirelessly argumentative on apparently minor points, a watchdog who knows all the rules of procedure and precedents, a diplomat who seeks a formula to reconcile opponents, an elder statesman who speaks late in the discussion, and the silent members who nod and vote. They all, even the last category, have a part to play, and their occasional usefulness is grudgingly admitted even by the people they irritate most; they are filling group roles as well as exercising personal idiosyncrasies. In the same way, school classes surprisingly often produce the more or less stereotyped figures of bright boy, bad boy, clown, bookworm, prig, athlete, teacher's pet, and this is understandable enough in view of the fairly similar values within reach of a group of schoolboys and the fairly similar assortment of personalities that it includes. But there is not likely to be a readymade fit between individual personality and group role; each will modify the other. The individual may greatly modify the conventional role. Or he may give way to group pressures and conform closely to a stereotype that only imperfectly expresses his personal qualities. In some cases he may be filling a role almost against his will, the role for instance of butt or buffoon, rather than be without a distinctive place in the group.

Certain aspects of the structure of groups which affect the emergence of leaders and the spread of individual influence within the group were brought to light by the 'sociometric' work of Moreno (1934). He recorded the attractions and antipathies found among small groups of children and adolescents, and displayed graphically the network of friendships within the group and the relative popularity and isolation of the individual members. Some of the more intimate psychological processes involved in defining oneself within a social group are likely to be better known as a result of studies in group psychotherapy which have been going on for many years (cf. Burrow, 1927, Slavson, 1950 and Bion, 1961). Here, under pressure generated by the need for help with his difficulties and in the relative security created by the clinical setting, the individual gains (and discloses) more insight into his response to social pressures and elicitations than he normally can in everyday groups. The roles that he takes the group to be offering or denying him and the means by which he finds himself evading or claiming them are among the discoveries that such a setting makes possible.

The same broad conception of a group's definition of roles as it copes with a particular situation, and the emergence of some member to fill each role, provided the basis for the well-known methods used by the War Office Selection Boards as part of the technique for identifying men who were likely to be effective and acceptable officers (cf. Harris, 1949). In outline, the method was to confront a leaderless group with a series of tasks demanding co-ordinated effort of various kinds, while observers noted what roles the individual members were inclined to take in the group's work and how far they were welcomed in those roles by the rest of the group.

There can be little doubt that this method of selection and the theoretical account of leadership that has supported it and developed with it are reflections of a gradual change in democratic countries in the background of opinion about leadership. The first German War helped to discredit the elders in England, and in some other belligerent countries, and encouraged the revolt of the nineteen-twenties both against upper-class claims to a monopoly of national leadership and against paternalistic direction in general. The extravagances of the leadership cult in the totalitarian countries further encouraged scepticism about leaders. These things helped to ensure receptive attention for psycho-analytic accounts of the more obscure and less creditable processes uniting a leader and his followers. The leader's craving for the sort of power attributed to the patriarchal father, the possibility that the yearning for power derives (as Suttie suggests) from the affection-hungry child's wish to extort love by force, the Adlerian theme of power-seeking as a compensation for real or imagined inferiority, such ideas all tended to undermine the simpler idea of leadership; if we still wanted leaders, they must be of a different kind from this. Equally the credit of the follower was undermined. The Freudian view that the leader was a father-figure to whom childish attitudes of dependence could be trans-ferred, and through whom individual responsibility could be shed and the discomfort of uncertainty evaded, was too convincing to be resisted, and its direct application to political affairs by Fromm (1942) gave it wider currency and strengthened its effect. As a political scientist, Lasswell (1949) attempted an analysis of the factors, including unconscious needs, which tend to impel people towards positions of leadership and power, taking the view that although the anarchist ideal of getting rid of power is exceedingly remote, yet the task of democracy is to chasten power and ensure its subordination to respect for human dignity.

While these general views were gaining currency the idea of dominative or paternalistic leadership in the practical affairs of industry was being abandoned by the more enlightened industrialists. They created the conditions and opportunities in the nineteen-twenties that allowed Mary Parker Follett (cf. Metcalf and Urwick, 1941), for instance, to elaborate in terms of everyday industrial life the view that the leader should be deriving his influence and power from his team's recognition that he was fulfilling functions of their own for them. She pointed out the inadequacies of the notions then current in psychology that traits of 'ascendancy' or assertiveness were of crucial importance for leaders. She distinguished between the 'leadership of personality' (i.e. of assertive personality) and the 'leadership of function', stating her belief that the latter was be-coming the more important. Her views and the climate of opinion that created an audience for them helped to set the scene for the newer ideas of industrial supervision that are associated with the work of Elton Mayo, T. N. Whitehead and others at the Hawthorne Works of the Western Electric Company in Chicago (cf. Roethlisberger and Dickson, 1949, Mayo, 1933, Whitehead, 1936). Probably the greatest value of psychological studies of leadership has been their justification and encouragement of this view that the leader's authority should be derived mainly from the functions he is performing for the group he controls rather than from any coercive force, whether of his personal domination or of some external authority who appointed him. This point of view is not only expressed in recent developments in industrial foremanship but has to some extent affected the notion of discipline in the fighting services and the nursing profession, previously strongholds of authoritarian leadership. The essence of it is the recognition that functional leadership neither implies nor confers any general personal superiority and that the subordinate is not an inferior. Needless to say, the adoption of that view in the abstract is of little use without the ability to convey it convincingly through the realities of social contact; and these realities include such things as forms of words and tones of voice that are not easily compassed by those who have grown up with the older ideas of authority.

Functional leadership is of special importance as being compatible with the growth and extension of non-authoritarian forms of social organisation. In ordinary English life, for example, unquestioned acceptance of the functional authority of the skipper of a fishing boat or the foreman of a mixed farm has brought with it little in the way of obsequiousness to him in the pub or deference to him in local politics. George Orwell (1938) records the gradual discovery by the anarchist troops in the Spanish Civil War that an entire absence of leadership was not only unworkable but was not necessary to their central principles; and they reached the position of accepting officers in the front line though giving them no marks of deference off-duty.

In this broad development of thought about leadership it is not always easy to see what specific contribution psychologists have made. They have, it is true, applied useful techniques in the selection and training of the newer kind of leader in industry and the fighting services, and the Hawthorne inquiry produced fairly conclusive evidence under experimental conditions that the new style of supervision leads to greater working efficiency. But one cannot help suspecting that in their thinking about leadership, as about many of the complex social questions, psychologists have themselves been profoundly influenced by contemporary currents of feeling, and that their view—correct as one hopes it is—may have been arrived at to some extent by rationalisations of what in any case they were going to believe. A courageous and well-known attempt to put some part of the current view about leadership to experimental test reveals the subtlety of the difficulties faced by the scientific investigator who is inevitably embedded in his own culture.

Lewin, Lippitt and White (1939) report a part of their now classic experiment which was concerned with the effects of different styles of leadership on the amount of aggression occurring in small groups. With small clubs of boys engaged in craft work they compared the effects of three kinds of adult control: authoritarian, democratic and what they called *laissez-faire*, which amounted to an absence of imposed authority. The essence of the method was the systematic recording of all the hostile actions and remarks that occurred in the clubs during each fifty-minute meeting, and a comparison between one group and another in terms of the number of these hostile incidents that occurred. They seem to have come about as near to objectivity as we could expect in an inquiry of this sort. Instead of general impressions which could be secured with a less elaborate experimental framework, they obtained an objective indication of levels of aggressiveness and expressed it numerically.

What were the results? They were that in terms of the numerical assessment the level of aggression was on the whole far lower with authoritarian leadership than with the other kinds. Could we not claim this as a sound scientific conclusion? If Lewin had been living contentedly in a totalitarian state he would almost certainly have left it at that and congratulated himself on the striking support his convictions had received from the strictest experimental investigation. Surely scientists with a bias towards authoritarian regimes

D*

might plausibly claim that Lewin *should* have left it at that or at least left the emphasis on his numerical results, since they gave the nearest approach to impartiality and objectivity of all the records he could make.

But Lewin was an exile from an authoritarian regime, living in the United States and loyal to the democracy he found there. He went beyond the numerical results of his experiment and reported very interesting qualitative observations strongly suggesting that the freedom from acts of aggression under authoritarian leadership went with a rather crushed, apathetic spirit among the boys, and reflected only the restrictive influence of the leader. In the discussion of the results the whole emphasis is placed on the relatively intangible advantages of democratic control, and not on the numerical results from which the greatest promise of scientific rigour had seemed to come. The case illustrates the familiar difficulty that in many psychological inquiries the psychologist has to decide at what point to end his investigation and report his findings. For example, the early investigators of possible racial and national differences in intelligence left us with the impression of there being fairly well-marked and reliable differences, and their reports of those results might well have enjoyed respect and oblivion in the technical journals. But because the practical implications were so great, for immigration policy and the treatment of minorities, they were gone over with a fine-tooth comb, the data re interpreted, the experimental work repeated and extended, and all sorts of over-looked complexities and subtleties brought to light, with the result that the early findings were largely discarded and we now have a clearer view of a very complex problem. It would be hard to show that it was the principles of experimental science which ensured that vitally important re-examination of the data; what led to it were the political scruples and social conscience of many psychologists.

In the complex matter of leadership it seems doubtful whether we have yet reached a reliable psychological analysis (let alone an experimental demonstration) that is independent of social assumptions and current trends in political thought. In practice, obviously, the desire for power and prestige still forms a large part of the motives of many who secure positions of leadership. Much theoretical discussion also implies that this is the only motive worth considering. Lasswell (1949) bases his analysis on that supposition. Krech and Crutchfield (1948) say that people with 'insistent needs for dominance, power, prestige' have 'higher potentiality for leadership', especially if they are used to satisfying those needs by 'dominating interpersonal relations with others'. LaPiere and Farnsworth (1949), having accepted the unsatisfactory definition of a leader as one whose behaviour affects others more than theirs affects his, are led to regard the issuing of orders to servants as leadership. Although a different conception of leadership is emerging in several areas of psychological work, the differences between one kind and another still need clarifying.

It seems doubtful whether the fact that a man influences others more than any one of them influences him should make us speak of him as a leader. The person of eminent achievement in technical invention or the arts, for instance, may influence others decisively, but by bringing them the more or less finished product of more or less solitary work. This is a most valuable form of co-operation (as we need to insist in these days of team-worship), but it is not the intimate co-operation from stage to stage in the task which is involved in leadership. The term 'leader' in a strict sense might profitably be kept for one who guides and co-ordinates the efforts of a number of people (or at least one other person) while they perform some activity.

Further, it seems unsatisfactory to confuse the leader with the master or boss who merely uses others as instruments for increasing his own resources and furthering his private purposes. The research director who assembles a 'team' of assistants who for pay or Ph.D.s carry out a research programme of his private devising is not a leader but a boss. He may, however, move towards leadership if he discovers a satisfaction in contributing to a modified research programme that expresses the interests of the team and not merely his own. We can add, therefore, that a leader is one who guides and co-ordinates the efforts of a number of people to achieve an end that they have in common. The character of the leadership situation is decisively affected by the extent to which the members of the team have themselves taken part in defining their task, or the extent to which, if it is externally imposed, the leader can make its demands intelligible and acceptable to them in terms of the values they recognise. The latter process is, of course, immensely important in securing satisfactory morale among teams in the fighting services and nursing, at points where established demands and forms of discipline are not self-evidently justified by the obvious requirements of the job that the team came together to do. To the extent that the team fails to feel that the task it performs is its own task, the man in charge approaches the mere boss or master and loses the quality of leader.

Below many diversities of technique in leadership lies a basic difference in the leader's emphasis: whether on the task to be carried out by the team or on the members of the team as people having human value in themselves apart from their usefulness in the task. If he is absorbed exclusively in the former he will tend to diminish his team to the status of tools for the job. Such leaders may be of the utmost value for some tasks and in some circumstances, but between them and their team they generally need a buffer who is more sensitive to the team as individual human beings, who will consider the possibility of modifying any excessive demands of the job, and who will be more aware of the team's need for appreciation, encouragement and sympathy in difficulties. On the other hand, to be too much concerned with members of the team as people, and too little with the impersonal demands of the job, makes for ineffectual leadership or for the over-personal paternalistic kind in which pleasing the leader and remaining in his good books, by whatever means, become more important than contributing effectively to the task. Each leader can be viewed as standing somewhere between the extremes of absorption in the task and absorption in the team.

A third possibility, that the leader is unconsciously preoccupied less with the task or the team than with the importance for his own personality of being a leader, accounts for some of the more blatant failures. It helps to produce the leader who is touchy and self-important, who cannot delegate, who can tolerate only docile feeble helpers, who insists unduly on outward signs of deference, who has no competent deputy to take over in his absence, who is irreplaceable when he retires. A less serious over-concern with the significance of the role, at the cost of the task and the team, is a common temporary difficulty resulting from promotion. The newly promoted leader is insecure until he discovers whether his personality will fit the unfamiliar role, and the more the role has been defined in the older fashion of leadership the greater the insecurity will be.

For a time, undoubtedly, leadership will continue to be a topic of practical importance. And yet, whether as a social technique or a psychological concept, it is an unsatisfactory expedient, due to be superseded. An alternative concept, of distinctive roles, all necessary to the task of the group and none carrying total or permanent pre-eminence, is available from studies of the way small groups, without an assigned leader, actually perform tasks (cf. Cattell, 1951 and Cartwright and Zander, 1960).

But techniques of social organisation, lagging far behind psychological concepts, still make for fixity and totality of leadership. Because one member of a group is likely to direct it best in many of its tasks he is expected (and himself expects) to take charge of all. Such things as differences of pay and hierarchial status confirm the fixed role. They stand in the way of techniques based on the distribution of function and responsibility among members of a working group according to the capacities of each, with frequent shifts in the locus of initiative and influence as phases of the group's undertaking vary. In conventional leadership, uneasiness arises in the leader himself and in the others if he ceases to lead. We have few techniques for institutionalising and facilitating shifts in leadership so as to allow a temporary leader to shed his role without loss of face and without undermining the confidence of others in him on appropriate occasions. It may be that the necessary social devices will develop step by step with the discovery, especially in small working groups, that equal co-operation, with role-shift as the tasks change, is a practicable and efficient alternative to fixed leadership.

The emergence of alternative techniques to leadership will be slow because it depends on a high level of psychological security in all members of the group. What has become known, since the pioneering study by Adorno *et al.* (1950), as the authoritarian personality forms a large proportion of our populations and provides not only willing leaders but eager followers. And apart from those special factors of parent–child relation that help to form the extreme authoritarian personality, there will always be difficulties in passing from the inevitable dependence of childhood to an adult relationship that is something other than a modified or disguised form of the child–adult pattern. Adolescent rebelliousness, so repetitive in spite of its surface variety generation after generation, brings no change, since it supports itself within the framework against which it kicks. But slow as the development of more flexible techniques of non-dominative co-operation may be, it is to them that we must look for the alternative to leadership which Trotter, in the magnificent and prophetic 'Postscript of 1919' (to the later editions of *Instincts of the Herd in Peace and War*), viewed as our sole hope:

'If society is to continue to depend for its enterprise and expansion upon leadership, and can find no more satisfactory source of moral power, it is, to say the least, highly probable that civilisations will continue to rise and fall in a dreadful sameness of alternating aspiration and despair until perhaps some lucky accident of confusion finds for humanity in extinction the rest it could never win for itself in life.'

10

THE SOCIAL MEANING OF NORMALITY

For social psychology and psychotherapy alike the concept of 'normality' is crucial and stands by implication in the background of all discussions of social development, culture patterns and their deviants, and mental health. It has, however, received little explicit attention. We speak readily of abnormality but the contrasting norm is something that we leave everyone to understand for himself. The fact is that the notion belongs first and foremost to common speech and ordinary thinking and to the social wisdom that our language makes accessible. Whatever special study we may make of it, we are bound to abstract and distinguish among aspects of a much richer, if confused, conception in use for the everyday purposes of our social life.

The easiest aspect of the total concept to handle separately is its statistical implication, the suggestion that most of us are normal and that the normal is in some way related to the usual. Yet, clear as it is, this idea can be applied only with the utmost caution. The wariness with which responsible psychologists use it is seen in the remark of Culpin and Smith (1930) when they were engaged in sorting out psycho-neurotic workers from the others; these others they described in the following cautious terms:

'At one extremity is the emotionally well-poised, sensitive and highly intelligent man, at the other is the rather dull person [both being free from psycho-neurotic symptoms]. It has not been considered desirable to call

this group "normal" as that implies more knowledge than we have.
With increasing knowledge it may be possible to get some conception of
the "mode", i.e., the commonest type in a random sample of the population.'

It is true that with vastly increased knowledge we might eventually state every aspect of a man in terms of his deviation from the
average or from the mode of some selected series of people, such
as the population of a nation. We could say that he was of average
height and speed of movement, slept ten per cent longer than the
average, and worked five per cent less; that he was modal in being
uncannibalistic but belonged to a class of vegetarians who comprised
such and such a proportion of the population. But anything approaching a complete account of a person's psychological characteristics
on these lines would be unworkably cumbrous.

The statistical conception of normality is clear and intellectually
respectable. Moreover, it is likely to be somewhere in the background in most contexts in which the term is used, even though
other criteria are present too. But it falls far short of what the popular conception implies. For one thing it ignores the fact that in
popular usage to judge a man normal or abnormal places him in a
particular relation with his social group. The statistical conception
places him only in terms of a statistical series; it fails to bring out
the fact that the array of people of which he forms part is associated
socially as well as statistically.

Quite evidently the notion of normality has some connection
with the prevailing judgements of value, and this alone sets it
apart from merely statistical facts. A man can have unusual strength
and courage, a woman can have unusual beauty and, nowadays,
intelligence, without being regarded as abnormal. That term is
usually the stigma of something undesirable; it will seldom be
incurred by exceptional development in an approved direction.

But the connection between the value judgements and the idea of
the normal is complex. Although we usually regard good characteristics as normal we readily distinguish between bad behaviour and
abnormal behaviour. To call a man an extraordinary scoundrel or
an egregious fool takes note in passing of the statistical fact that
there are not many like him, but it by no means implies that he

is abnormal; in fact, if we can be persuaded to consider him abnormal our view of his bad or stupid behaviour is changed—we
say 'perhaps he is not responsible'.

Here one touches on the most important function of the concept in group life. Putting it in general terms, we can say that to
judge behaviour as abnormal is in some degree to deny it social
relevance. In the ordinary way, every action and thought which
we reveal has social significance: in some degree, however slight, it
sanctions or challenges the behaviour and judgements of others in
our group. It imperceptibly confirms existing usages by conforming,
or it questions them by deviating from what is established. So long
as we admit our companion to be normal his behaviour has implications for our standards of judgement; he forms part of the network of reciprocally sanctioning and challenging personalities
which makes up a social group. If his behaviour is specially fine it
tends to raise the standards by which we judge ourselves and others.
Bad conduct or foolishness of opinion, if it were tolerated, would
tend to lower our standards. And to protect them we bring to bear
on the offender various social pressures such as pleading, dissuasion,
ridicule, withdrawal of respect and liking, or perhaps material
punishment.

But in certain circumstances, which must be examined later, it
seems useless or needless to apply social pressures to the offender.
Instead, we make the judgement that he is abnormal. We may still
lock him up or otherwise prevent repetition of the behaviour, but
we do so as we would lock up a dangerous bull or confine the
waters of a flooding river; our aim is only self-protection by
material means. We have no hope that social pressure or punishment
can in this case bring the offender to seek a more satisfactory social
relationship with us by modifying his behaviour. What we
essentially do by the judgement of abnormality is to insulate the
social group from the effects of the offender's example. This practical function in group life of the idea of normality is the first thing
to be insisted on, whatever problems remain about the criteria of
normality.

The fact that the judgement of abnormality exempts the individual from ordinary social criticism and pressures is only half the

story. The other aspect of the judgement, less explicit but in some ways far more important, is that the deviant individual and his actions, once having been judged abnormal, are not socially disturbing and need not be taken seriously as a challenge to current standards and beliefs.

For instance, if one of our friends washes his hair twice a week when we wash ours once, we may wonder whether his example ought to be followed. The difference between his behaviour and our own is socially relevant. If, however, another friend has a compulsion to wash his hands repeatedly, however clean they may be, at very short intervals throughout the day, his behaviour has no force for us as an example or a challenge; we judge it to be abnormal, and so make it socially irrelevant in the sense I have suggested. We may or may not know it to be a recognised psychoneurotic symptom, but one way or another we feel confident in putting it outside the social context. Again, moderate thrift in our companions may strike us as an example that we wish we could follow, but the thrift of the miser has no significance for us; we exclude him from social relevance by the judgement of abnormality.

It can be seen that the device of labelling a mode of conduct or a belief as abnormal—or as one of the milder forms of the same quality, such as odd, cranky, fanatical or eccentric—may provide a tool in the service of conservative trends in society. Where persecution would give an innovator the advantage of martyrdom, the suggestion that he is cranky or crazy is sometimes used to greater effect. In particular, it is used while the main group still feels safe and comfortably superior. This can be seen in the history of the abolition of the slave trade. Summing up the attitude of the merchants of Liverpool towards the early advocates of abolition, Averil Mackenzie-Grieve (1941) writes:

'To [the Liverpool merchants] such men as Rathbone and Roscoe were enigmas. Business men and prosperous, the slave traders felt them to be victims of a morbid and foolish fanaticism and their opinions were utterly discounted.'

However, the judgement of abnormality may in one way aid

the innovator and contribute to the potential plasticity of a social group. To be called cranky and then left alone gives a minority idea some chance of survival which it might not have if it were taken seriously. In this sense the judgement of abnormality becomes, within certain limits, a technique of toleration and a source of protection for deviant individual opinion. A complex society like ours has a sort of waste-paper basket crammed with beliefs and minority practices which it doesn't bother ever to argue against, doesn't try to extinguish, perhaps hasn't ever made up its mind about, but from which it insulates itself by ascribing to them some degree of oddity or abnormality. Adherents of the flat-earth theory, nudists, opponents of vaccination, believers in the zymotic causation of disease, and endless other eccentrics are encapsulated within the social tissue and made irrelevant by being pronounced cranky. Among them they may be preserving some few beliefs that will turn out to be of the utmost value, and while the label 'cranky' or 'abnormal' denies them contemporary effectiveness it will also preserve them from the annihilating pressure of a really hostile group.

What that pressure may be is again seen in the history of the slave trade: when the movement for abolition became really formidable, Clarkson, a zealous abolitionist, began to receive anonymous threats and warnings and one attempt on his life was actually made. And a Liverpool doctor who adhered to the abolitionist cause found that his patients left him in protest (Mackenzie-Grieve, 1941). Had such pressures been exerted at an earlier stage, when the weak cause was still treated as a harmless aberration, they might have been dangerously effective.

The judgement of abnormality is an extreme form of social insulation. In that light it can be seen as a special case of the more familiar social device of limiting the significance of certain kinds of behaviour by setting them apart as a permitted licence in some section of the community. We do this in the case of children, taking for granted in them behaviour that we might regard as folly or crime or wild abnormality in adults. Again, each sex develops its own psychological characteristics, looking upon those of the other as peculiarities to be tolerated. But once a kind of behaviour has been classed as abnormal it is put more decisively outside the social context than these.

We have next to try to separate the entangled ideas that influence a particular society's current conception of what is normal. Among them will undoubtedly be the biological inheritance of the people and the effect of such environmental factors as climate, diet, chemical constitution of the available water, the diseases endemic in the region, and so on. The resultant human material which the culture has to shape will, for these reasons, vary in some ways from one group to another; the level of intelligence may differ, the proportion of old people to young, the average age at puberty, and many similar factors, all having their effect on the range of characteristics that the group regards as normal.

In certain fundamentals the concept of normality in every viable social group will correspond to the biologist's view of what is normal in an animal species. In particular various extreme peculiarities (or 'perversions') of sexual appetite and food appetite must be regarded as abnormal; otherwise the group would die out. But to a limited number of members of any group, a range of choice which ignores the simpler biological promptings may be permitted and regarded as unusual but not in the popular sense abnormal. Thus, among us, the individual choice of celibacy is not regarded as evidence of abnormality; nor is the willingness to die for a cause or an ideal. In fact, the biological fundamentals will not give many clues to the value-choices which a group comes to regard as normal. Nor will they suggest why certain human potentialities are developed further in one group than another, the particular degree of development being in each case considered normal, and stabilised by the group's institutions and customary beliefs and sentiments.

Undoubtedly, the most important aspect of the everyday conception of normality is that which sees it as being conterminous with sanity, the view that identifies the abnormal with the psychopathological. In earlier centuries, so it seems to us, the distinction between insanity and mental health was made more readily and seemed altogether simpler than it does now. The flagrant madman was recognised, but slighter forms of mental disorder seem not to have brought exemption from ordinary social pressures. Everyone but the lunatic was 'responsible'. The term 'responsible' raises difficult ethical, theological and legal questions. But in this present psychological context it is simpler. To say that almost everyone was treated as responsible amounts to saying that almost everyone was treated as a social being whose actions were to be interpreted as if they meant whatever they would have meant if you had carried them out yourself. You judged what motive would have led *you* to do what your companion did, and you assumed that he must have had the same motive. You then meted out friendliness or antagonism accordingly.

The characteristic of the madman was the patent impossibility of attributing any understandable motive to his actions. What he did was unaccountable in terms of one's own motivation, however wicked or imprudent one's impulses might be. The madman, therefore, was gradually recognised as being cut off from the social context. His actions might make him a physical menace—and lead to drastic restraints and perhaps irrational revenges—but once he was recognised as mad he was no longer a social menace, there was no possibility that his standards of conduct would challenge the moral traditions or the customs of the group. Nor, it was gradually seen, was deterrent punishment relevant. No one could be tempted to follow his example, for it was unaccountable, expressing no conceivable motivation.

This is one of the most important of the criteria that guide our verdict of normality, that we believe we can spontaneously comprehend some motivation for the normal person's actions. We may, in fact, be wrong about it, but at least a possible motivation presents itself. We cannot in this way put ourselves into the abnormal person's place and feel that we know why he acted as he did. In such cases, where spontaneous imaginative insight is baffled, we have to resort to some secondary intellectual process to account for the odd action: at one time we spoke of possession by a spirit, and nowadays psychopathology offers more detailed explanations. In either case we need some effort of reasoning, something beyond the spontaneous insight by which we judge the meaning of the ordinary person's behaviour.

Although our view of the abnormal is so much influenced by the work of psychopathologists, it would be over-optimistic to suppose that the technique of psychiatry or the science of psychopathology had been guided by a clear conception of normality. Much of the time they have been concerned with such extreme deviations from average or modal behaviour that their patients were grossly handi-capped in leading everyday lives in their ordinary social setting, and it was enough for the practitioner to bring them back nearer to the mode of the group. In assessing recovery from serious dis-orders the physician has been guided more by the expectations of his group than by principles drawn from his own special science.

Yet modern psychopathologists have clarified the central criterion of mental health and therefore one of the essential ideas in the every-day notion of normality. They have shown that much mental ill-health expresses the mind's failure to achieve or maintain integration. A great part of the abnormal behaviour that is marked by incom-prehensibility of motive is shown to be capable of explanation in terms of unconscious distortions or deflections of motive. The unaccountable actions and failures to act, the queer interests and inexplicable emotions, the delusions, and so on, have a significance in the total mental economy of the person which is concealed from his conscious self. His mind is to that extent divided against itself and failing to maintain its wholeness. Parts of it that are influencing his actions and feelings are nevertheless not within the purview, nor within the control, of the organised hierarchy of interests and sentiments which the person has come to regard as his 'self'.

If, then, we are thinking of abnormality as a degree of mental disorder (or some condition short of full mental health), we have, as a hypothetical extreme opposite, the concept of a whole or integrated mind. No such mind exists, that need hardly be said. But this hypothetical perfection is implicit as the extreme opposite of the sort of abnormality which results from dissociation or repression or some other form of self-deception through un-conscious processes.

It must not be thought that the whole or integrated mind would be one without conflict. A complex organism living in a complex environment must inevitably experience conflict in the sense that aspects of one and the same situation will often arouse incompatible impulses and some process of choice must occur before action can take place. That happens at lower levels of the nervous system, and neurologists such as Sherrington (1906) have shown that when incompatible reflexes are stimulated simultaneously an inhibitory process will check the one so that the other can occur. Selective inhibition of responses is an essential feature of the integrative action of the nervous system.

A parallel process at higher levels of mental life, involving the conscious rejection of one impulse, is equally an essential feature of the integrated mind. The process of choice and conscious rejection, as many psychopathologists have pointed out, is entirely different from repression, in which the conscious self loses awareness of, and control over, the repressed impulse. There is much to be said for keeping the term 'inhibition' to describe the process of consciously checking an impulse; such a use would suggest the parallel with the perfectly healthy and normal process at lower neural levels.

Whatever terms we employ it seems clear that integration in mental life is far from implying the absence of conflict between desires. Conscious tension and the conscious need for choice are *signs* of integration. The fact that we experience tension between an impulse and some opposed sentiment means that we are holding the incompatibles together in a complex mental whole. From such conscious conflict arises the possibility of development. For that reason, one must question MacCurdy's (1939) suggestion that a fully integrated mind would be static and incapable of further development; this would be true only if one took integration to imply absence of conflict (apart from all question of development to meet the challenge of environmental changes).

The ideal of an integrated mind, free from unconscious deflections of motive, and able to tolerate conscious conflict, is implied in a paper on the normal mind by Ernest Jones (1942), who concludes that the basic clinical feature of normality is freedom from unconscious anxiety and its various disguises. It seems evident that unconscious anxiety, although perhaps of fundamental importance clinically, is in fact only one manifestation of the general process by which some parts of what could have been mental life are repressed or are prevented from ever reaching consciousness.

The notion of reducing the necessity for repression and bringing to consciousness more of what is potentially conscious is the most important contribution that psychopathology has made to the conception of normality. Its importance lies partly in the fact that it refers simply to a psychological process, not a process of selection by ethical criteria. What is brought to light must inevitably be subject to the value judgements of the individual but the process of bringing to light implies only the judgement that an integrated mind is preferable to a self-deceiving mind.

The view that repression is in principle undesirable is not accepted by all psycho-analysts. Glover (1933), for example, believes that some repression of primitive impulse is desirable and constitutes a legitimate means of flight from an inner danger. Moreover, psycho-analysis as a whole has blurred the picture by the idea of sublimation, according to which some forms of substitutive or symbolic gratification of unacceptable impulses are to be welcomed—largely because they have social approval for their outcome. In spite of much writing on the subject, it still seems uncertain whether sublimation and repression differ by psychological, as distinct from ethical, criteria. If not, the analysts are inevitably thrown back on their own ethical judgement, or on mere conformity to current social standards, in deciding which unconscious distortions of motive they should encourage and which they should help to eliminate.

But whatever the views of clinicians, it is clear that in theory we have a psychological, and not necessarily an ethical, concept in that of the integrated personality. The status in ethics of a preference for a whole mind rather than a self-deceiving mind is not a question directly for psychology, though it seems difficult to suppose that moral behaviour achieved through self-deception can be entirely satisfactory in any ethical system.

For social psychology two points have to be made. Firstly, if we believe that unconscious distortions of motive are largely responsible for our companion's behaviour or convictions we minimise his social significance by calling him abnormal. Secondly, convictions and ways of life dismissed on these grounds may none the less be valuable to more normal minds and may be justified by way of normal mental processes. The orthodox and conventional may insulate themselves against an uncomfortable challenge by pointing out quite incontrovertibly that the man who presents it is highly abnormal and that his beliefs are inextricably intertwined with his abnormalities. But what the main body of contemporary opinion may dismiss in this way, normal people may later on find to be of immense value, as for instance in the cases of George Fox and William Blake.

In some degree, unconscious distortion of motive is common to us all. It has, therefore, to have gone very far before behaviour strikes us as really incomprehensible, and as being abnormal in the sense of having to be exempted from ordinary social appraisal. This fact throws some light on the curious attempt which some people have made to regard all crime as abnormal. In the sense that it will nearly always arise from processes that involve some unconscious distortion of motive, that it will imply a personality poorly integrated in some respects, crime is no doubt nearly always abnormal. But it is not so abnormal in that sense that it becomes genuinely incomprehensible to the rest of us. Some of it really is. A devoted mother who, during a bout of depression, kills her children in order to spare them the misery of living is abnormal in the sense that her actions are incomprehensible without the specialised knowledge of psychopathology. On the other hand, a man who kills another man in order to prevent the exposure of a black-market organisation is not in the least incomprehensible. Some kinds of theft are so pointless and incomprehensible, without special knowledge of kleptomania, that most people can genuinely view them as abnormal. Other thefts are perfectly comprehensible to most of us; they represent short cuts of the kind that we have learnt to avoid and deplore, but which we cannot pretend not to understand.

When direct imaginative insight fails to make a person's conduct comprehensible, and we have to resort to secondary thought processes and intellectual hypotheses before we can glimpse a motive, then we can reasonably call him abnormal. But a community that claimed to see all crime as abnormal in this sense would either be remarkably saintly or else would be flattering itself.

Among the many conceptions confusedly present in the everyday use of the words normal and abnormal the conception of the degree of integration and freedom from self-deception possessed by a mind is probably the most important. It implies that a mind which differs widely from what is usual in the social group may nevertheless be nearer normality in this sense than many orthodox minds. It is true that the development of such a mind will have depended on the materials and potentialities offered by the culture in which it lived, and there will be wide differences between a well-integrated mind in one culture and an equally well-integrated mind in another. But the possibility presents itself that those minds in each culture which are most normal, in the sense of being most nearly whole and coherent, would find more common ground than the conventional and in Trotter's sense 'resistive' minds of the various cultures can.

Evidence is hard to come by but it seems probable that some cultures distort, more than others, certain constitutional qualities of human nature. The intense mutual suspicion and hostility of the islanders of Dobu, the withdrawn detachment of the Balinese, probably depend on pathological processes that interfere with a more natural tendency to value affection. The institutions and sentiments of mediaeval chivalry, as it affected the relations between the sexes, did violence to human nature. The Victorian conceptions of decency meant too serious a distortion of natural facts to be maintained without repression. It seems likely that a well-integrated mind will tend to strain away from those features of its culture which too much distort human nature and which would involve severe conflict but for rationalisation and repression. If there is such a thing as human nature, a range of psychological potentiality made actual in different degrees by the various cultures, our chances of learning about it will depend on studying the deviants as well as the conventional members of human societies.

In summary, it seems likely that there are some basic characteristics of human-nature-in-society which will make themselves felt in any relatively well-integrated mind. But, thanks to our speech and our tool-making abilities and our social inheritance, there is also a vast range of possible activity and experience from which each different culture, and within that culture each individual mind, makes its choice. It will thus be normal for cultures and individual people to differ very widely, so that human normality, far from being uniform, includes immense variety.

Every culture is engaged in a perpetual defence of its established values, and those individuals who deviate from its usual level of attainment or its usual range of value judgements are under social pressure to return to conformity. But if the individual's deviation seems to his companions to be due to constitutional inadequacies of equipment or to a distintegration or confusion of mind that makes his motive incomprehensible, they are then likely to judge him abnormal and thus to insulate themselves from him socially. Implicit in the judgement of normality there is also concern for mental integration and coherence. But where a culture has stabilised behaviour based on morbid unconscious processes, some of its deviant individuals may be much nearer mental coherence than the conforming members of the group. Consequently the notion of normality as wholeness of mind may differ widely from the view of normality based on what happens to be current in a social group at a particular time. The possibility always remains, therefore, that among the deviant individuals excluded from the full social context are some who might well be accepted by their society as a challenge to self-criticism and the re-examination of values.

11

SOCIAL PLASTICITY AND INNOVATION

It seems probable that the continued existence of a social group demands, besides stability in the norms and institutions that define it, a great measure of plasticity. An over-rigid definition of acceptable practice and too narrow a concept of the normal seem often to be followed in a vigorous group by an expansionary tendency in which a neglected range of human experience comes to the fore again; a process seen, for instance, in the swings from 'classicism' to 'romanticism' in literature. The extent of the changes in socially sanctioned outlook that occur among compact primitive groups is not clear; apart from a few notorious and dramatic changes such as the Fijians' swings between warlike and peaceful institutions, the shifts between generation and generation in the culture patterns of primitive peoples have not been fully recorded and are not often studied closely by anthropologists (though see Majumdar, 1950). There are, on the other hand, instances in more complex societies of sub-groups that have become exceedingly rigid and, apparently as a consequence, have died out.

One example is provided by the Irish literary profession of *fili* in the twelfth and thirteenth centuries which developed out of the profession of sorcery (inheriting much of the prestige of the latter) and at first combined the functions of judges with those of poets. The profession was minutely classified into ranks, the *ollam* knowing three hundred and fifty stories, the *ánruth* one hundred and seventy-five, the *clii* eighty, the *cana* sixty, and so on; the stories were classified as primary and secondary, the latter being obligatory only on the higher ranks; and the most elaborate poem technically was the exclusive right of the *ollam*. The *fili* needed twelve years' training, which included the learning not only of legends, law, history, topography and grammar but also of highly complicated verse metres and obscure kennings. It seems that with this degree of specialisation and rigidity the profession contributed less and less to the contemporary life of the community, until by the sixteenth century the *fili* had become extinct and the homelier and once despised 'bard' served the literary needs of the society. Although it seems unlikely that in a case like this increasing rigidity would be the sole and simple cause of extinction, still the tendency for excessive rigidity to lessen the vigour and effectiveness of a group is probably at work both here and in less clear-cut instances.

Anthropologists and social psychologists have given most attention to the plasticity that allows one group to make cultural borrowings from another, and the broad principles that govern such borrowings are fairly clear. Elements of a foreign culture are accepted most easily when they demonstrably meet a recognised need of the borrowing culture more effectively than do the existing techniques; European colonisers found their fire-arms and other material goods more readily accepted than their moral code, social customs or religious beliefs. Religious systems are especially difficult to introduce from one culture to another, but the way is smoothed if they can be linked to a demonstrable superiority in some other social function; hence the success of medical missionaries and of such demonstrations as the superiority of Jehovah to Baal as a rain-giver.

Acceptance of a foreign element unchanged is comparatively rare, the usual process being one of modification and assimilation to the borrowing culture, a fact that was plain to the earliest observers. Lane Fox (1867) gives ample illustration of this principle in the borrowing of tools and weapons. He mentions that in Tahiti Captain Cook could not persuade the natives of the value of metal until his armourer had made an iron adze of exactly the same shape as their basalt adzes, after which they adopted metal tools, though to a great extent preserving the shape of the old ones. At the time Lane Fox wrote, the Fijians could get steel blades, chisels and axes from the traders, but preferred plane irons above all, since those resembled the ancient stone adzes of their own make and could be lashed to a handle in the same fashion; similarly, the Purus Indians of South America would break off the handle of a European knife, place the blade between two pieces of wood and bind it tight with a sinew, so making it like one of their native tools. He also records that during the American War of Independence, when the English wanted to arm some of the Indians as allies, they were obliged to make tomahawks to the native pattern with a pipe incorporated in the handle.

A parallel process in the assimilation of customs and beliefs is familiar in the Christianisation of earlier pagan festivals. St. Lucy, for example, was an early Christian who, on rejecting the advances of a Roman centurion, was covered with tar and set alight; but although the fire blazed the virgin was unharmed. This episode, as well as her name, thus associated her with light, making her in fact a torch. Her feast is on 13th December, the turning point after which the days begin to lengthen; and in Scandinavia, where the return of the light must always have had intense significance, it is kept with a light-bringing ceremony in which the household, assembled in a darkened room, greets a young girl who enters with a crown of lighted candles. The detailed processes by which this Christian story became fused with a solstice festival (and the reasons why the rejoicings of midsummer eve were not similarly Christianised) were no doubt intricate and may now be too remote in time for certain knowledge.

However, similar processes are always occurring, and recent examples are accessible to study. One of the well-documented instances is that examined by F. C. Bartlett (1923), using the original study by Radin, of the introduction of the peyote cult among the Winnebago Indians. For a full psychological account his excellent chapter on 'Psychological factors in the transmission of culture by borrowing' should be read, but an outline must be given here for the sake of the broad pattern it reveals, a pattern whose main features frequently recur in social innovation. The innovator, John Rave, had been brought up in the shamanistic cults of the Winnebago. On a visit to another district he met with the

ritual eating of the peyote (the button of a cactus which contains
the drug mescal) and convinced himself that it had curative
properties. He returned to his home among the Winnebago and
gradually introduced the cult to his relations, largely on the grounds
of its therapeutic value. At first, he was passive and unantagonistic
towards the older cults, but as the number of his converts grew a
new sub-group began to form around the peyote ceremonial and
tension developed between the conservative adherents of the older
shamanistic cults and the more radical converts to the new. One
convert, Hensley, who was more radical than Rave, introduced the
Christian Bible into the ceremonies, with other ideas and rites
borrowed from Christianity; the peyote, however, remained
central, being regarded as a means of inducing inspired interpretation of the Bible. As the new cult grew and gained more general
acceptance it was gradually assimilated to the older religious
practices. The more conservative members of the community interpreted the new ideas in terms of the old, the more radical reversed
the process. The former, for instance, decided that peyote-eating
gave the same magical powers as those conferred by membership
of the older cults' Medicine Dance; the latter identified the Trick-
ster, a character in the old myths, with the Satan of the new beliefs.
    Round this one new feature of peyote-eating, says Bartlett,

'gathered gradually many of the old observances and customs—a ceremonial
circuit of the lodge; two sacred peyote, one male, the other female; the
old sacred mound of the buffalo-dance; crossed lines on the earth; the
association of the peyote with the hearing of voices, a visit to the home of
God, the gift of song, the foretelling of events, and so on. Yet certain interpretations representing new Christian beliefs came in also: the mound was
interpreted as Mount Sinai; "the crossed lines as the cross with Christ
upon it, the ceremonial crook as the shepherd's crook, or as the rod with
which Moses smote the rock". These new interpretations, however, varied
from person to person as the old ones never did.'

As the new cult grew and Rave's personal ascendancy declined, so
the older cultural patterns asserted themselves more definitely.
    Whether a successful innovation is greatly modified by assimi-
lation to older features of the culture, or is ultimately accepted in

something like its original form, the striking fact is its final establishment as an orthodoxy. It then becomes difficult for even the most conservative people to believe that it ever provoked as much opposition as in fact it did. It almost seems, in fact, that the degree of initial disturbance is particularly difficult to appreciate when the new idea has been fairly recently assimilated to the conventional outlook. For us, probably, it is easy to understand, by a slight effort of historical imagination, the disturbing quality of the Reform Bill of 1832. The limitation of the powers of the House of Lords in 1910, however, we take rather for granted, and it comes as a surprise that W. J. Courthope, a Professor of English Poetry at Oxford, could be moved to say at the end of a six-volume *History of Poetry* (London, 1910):

'The great centrifugal movement in the life of the nation towards a visionary ideal of individual Liberty has drifted us, with little pilotage, down the stream of our destiny to a bifurcation of the river, and we must make our choice down which of the diverging arms the vessel of the State shall be navigated. As I lay down my pen we are being asked to decide whether or not we will abruptly take our leave of the great continuous traditions of the past.'

In a homelier matter, it is difficult now to realise at all fully the opposition aroused in the early nineteen-twenties by the wearing of shorts for cycling, even by men, let alone by women. A series of letters from cyclists (*C.T.C. Gazette*, 70, 2; February 1951) recalls the amount of feeling that could be aroused by that innovation:

'I recollect that it took a good deal of pluck before I actually left home in shorts, my habit being to get out of London and then change behind a hedge.'
'I remember that the ordinary dress of the club-girl in those days was very much like a pair of knickerbockers covered by a long coat to mid-calf or knickerbockers worn with a shorter coat like the old-type Norfolk jacket. . . . My wife rejected this stifling attire, and adopted shorts and a man's lightweight of those days. . . . We were greeted with yelps and catcalls, interest and disapproval, and a surprising amount of really good-natured banter from the general public.'

'I was two or three years later . . . in first wearing shorts for cycling and as I also wore an open-necked shirt, wags often made amusing remarks about "girls' clothes". . . . Some of the younger members may be surprised to know that it needed considerable courage to go out without a hat in the middle twenties. My parents were worried by the fact that they had a "crank" in the family, and sometimes I wondered whether the comfort was worth the ridicule.'

The hardening of the accepted innovation into a new orthodoxy is well illustrated by the attitude of G. T. Wrench, one of Lister's disciples. After the stubborn opposition of the medical profession to Lister's work had at last been broken, Wrench rigidly maintained that Lister's double cyanide gauze covered by carbolic-impregnated cotton-wool was 'final perfection' in dressings. He held that

'to "improve and modify" the completeness of genius is bound to terminate in a medley of confusion'.

According to Rhoda Truax (1947),

'some time after the Chief was dead Wrench continued to maintain that "man should confirm the inscrutable decrees of Providence, which pick out one man and endow him with supreme genius, by preserving his incomparable value in a firm tradition". Gravely he went on to deplore the "age in which liberty and progress as ideals have jealously destroyed the equally legitimate claims of authority and tradition".'

In the practical question of social change, there are two distinguishable problems. One arises from the simple fact that if a society is plastic enough to change at all it may change for the better or for the worse. Good things may be preserved by rigid custom and bad things introduced by social change; equally easily, custom may retain bad things and innovation bring in good. The preference that the individual members of the group express at each point of choice, the alternative they support, must reflect their system of values and the needs they recognise at the time. But this intrinsic difficulty about any choice is complicated by the possible existence in a social group of active tendencies, radical or conservative, which are making for or against innovation *qua* innovation. The

E

danger is of becoming partisan for the conservative or the innovating tendency as such and assuming that anything favoured by
the tendency we find congenial must therefore be good.

The practical problem has always been an important one for any
vigorous group. In his *Life of Samuel Johnson*, Boswell records that
in 1773 Johnson and some of his friends discussed the extent to
which a social group can tolerate unorthodox opinions held by its
individual members. Johnson claimed for the individual a rather
nebulous liberty of thought and then went on:

"But, Sir, no member of a society has a right to *teach* any doctrine
contrary to what the society holds to be true. The magistrate, I say, may be
wrong in what he thinks; but while he thinks himself right, he may and
ought to enforce what he thinks." Dr. Mayo, a dissenting minister, replied,
"Then, Sir, we are to remain always in error, and truth never can prevail;
and the magistrate was right in persecuting the first Christians." Johnson:
"Sir, the only method by which religious truth can be established is by
martyrdom. The magistrate has a right to enforce what he thinks; and he
who is conscious of the truth has a right to suffer. I am afraid there is no
other way of ascertaining the truth but by persecution on the one hand
and enduring it on the other." '

Beneath Johnson's manner of robust good sense there lurks the
underlying stupidity of not letting yourself see the full importance
of a problem because you have no solution. We still have no
solution. Some of our contemporaries, however, follow the nineteenth-century liberal trend in a more one-sided treatment of the
problem. Herbert Read (1934), for instance, asserts that

'from history in all its aspects, emerges the incontrovertible law which Mill
expressed in these words: "The initiation of all wise or noble things comes and
must come from individuals; generally at first from some one individual."
Or negatively: "The despotism of custom is everywhere the standing
hindrance to human advancement, being in unceasing antagonism to that
disposition to aim at something better than customary, which is called
according to circumstances, the spirit of liberty, or that of progress or
improvement." '

This is a happy hemiopia that manages not to see one horn of the
dilemma. For, of course, we have to add that the initiation of a great

many base and foolish things has also come from individuals. When a social group accepts a new direction the change may be for the better or for the worse and the inertia that obstructs valuable advances may also prevent calamitous retrogressions. We are left, as before, with the responsibility of individual moral choice in each situation as it arises; righteousness cannot be ensured by backing either the magistrate or the martyr through thick and thin.

In the middle of the twentieth century we probably tend to go back to the clear-sighted eighteenth-century view of the dilemma that Johnson expressed, but without his robust complacency. The magistrate may be right, the innovator may be right, they may both be partly right and partly wrong. What is important is that each should see his own view and the alternative as clearly as possible and should make his choice with the minimum of irrelevant prejudice, the minimum of confusion of mind, and the minimum of irrational anxiety at the thought of change. Efforts of mutual persuasion are, as Johnson saw, our only means of handling such a conflict. We differ from Johnson in recognising more fully the value of the social plasticity that depends on the innovator and in deploring more wholeheartedly the wasteful conflict that results from the ordinary magisterial hostility to change. Our approach to the problem is likely to lie through the study in some detail of innovations that have occurred in the past in order to understand better the psychological machinery of innovation and to detect some of the factors which, in distant perspective, seem to have been irrelevant to a pure and simple choice between things as they were and things as they became.

12

INNOVATORS

It would be lamentable to treat 'innovation' as a unitary topic,
suitable for broad psychological generalisations, in the way that
some of the older text-books of psychology treated 'leadership'.
The outstanding fact is the great variety of social processes associated
with innovation, and the few general statements that may be
hazarded must be treated with caution. It seems profitable to give
some attention to the personal qualities of innovators—not of 'the
innovator', but of a number of individual people who have brought
about a striking social change—as much to observe the wide
diversity of outlook and personality found among them as to notice
one or two characteristics that they seem to share. The innovators
to be considered here are of the kind who experience formidable
antagonism from their group, whether as active opposition or as
neglect; they do not include representatives of the large number
who carry forward some technical development (such as jet-
propulsion or atom-splitting) with a reasonable degree of support
and sympathy from their professional sub-group.

Where antagonism is aroused it often comes from the fact that
the innovator has been sensitive to some conflict of feeling or idea
that others around him have dealt with by resistance or rationalisation. The process can be seen, conveniently halted midway, in
an entry from *The Diaries of Lady Charlotte Guest* (1950), for 5th
September, 1845:

'. . . we passed through Windsor Forest, by Ascot Heath and through
Windsor and Eton. The former I had never seen before, the latter not since

Janry. 1828. When I thought of all the sorrows and temptations my poor boys would have to go through in that place I quite shuddered and prayed that assistance might be granted them from above. It seems a sad prospect, but everybody says it is the only way to bring up boys; and what is to be done? How can I, a poor weak woman, judge against all the world?'

This represents an abortive form of an effort towards social change; she is too conscious to be one of Trotter's simple 'resistives' but his 'voice of the herd' (her 'everybody says') is influential enough to deter her from any action beyond this private gesture. It is interesting to note the invocation of a deity at such a point of uncertainty and helplessness. Presumably that state of mind reported here by Lady Charlotte Guest provides, when it occurs in enough people, the intellectual climate in which more active efforts at change can thrive.

On general grounds it seems likely, further, that the active innovator, besides being indocile enough to reject his group's conventional interpretations of experience, will at the same time be social enough to feel a strong need of converting others to his point of view. He will not generally (though the case of Cézanne, to be discussed, is perhaps an exception) be content with going his own way in isolation. Nor will he work against his social group merely in his own interests as criminals and sub-criminal swashbucklers do. The combination of strong social needs with indocility to at least some social pressures seems to be a fairly common feature in the personality of the more dramatic innovators.

From this as well as other points of view, it is worth while examining the case of Manet, as described by Duret, and the processes through which his work led the way to a series of innovations in nineteenth-century European painting. A topic of great general interest illustrated by Manet's life is the relation between the innovator and the more diffuse social tendencies that make his work possible. As so often happens, Manet brought to a sharp focus a fairly widespread discontent with the old order. Traditional academic art had become increasingly lifeless, remote both from visual experience and from contemporary subject matter, and among the younger painters there was already a diffuse dissatisfaction and some tendency towards realism. Manet carried this tendency further and used scenes of everyday life and contemporary costume in his pictures, instead of rehashing classical and historical scenes. In 1863, when he was thirty-one, discontent with the hidebound juries of the official Salon was vocal enough slightly to shake the authorities, who gave way to the extent of arranging an exhibition of the pictures that had been rejected, the famous Salon des Refusés. Here the picture that gained most attention, mainly in the form of violent abuse, was Manet's 'Déjeuner sur l'herbe'.

It was attacked on two grounds. One was its disregard of established canons in the use of colour: it juxtaposed patches of light colour without separating them with gradations of darker tone, and it introduced reflected colour into the shadows, the whole effect striking the orthodox as a 'debauch of colour'. But by this alone it could hardly have achieved the notoriety that made it important in the history of the innovation. To the general public its more glaring and significant offence was its immorality, for it showed women in the nude and men in contemporary costume at a picnic. For the public of 1863 nudes were decent only in a classical or mythological setting.

Here, it would seem, we must recognise a gesture of defiance, perhaps not fully conscious, on Manet's part. The device of having nude women and men in contemporary dress *may* simply have seemed necessary to him pictorially, but it was hardly in line with his trend towards realism and he did not go on using it. It seems more likely that, already exasperated, he found a satisfaction in defying the conventional in this direction too and in sharpening the sense of difference between himself and the respectable orthodox. This is certainly what the picture achieved. It is as though Manet at this point decisively adopted a social role, the need for which had been gradually defined by gathering tension between two factions. What had been a rather diffuse and formless tension now focused itself around Manet; the malcontents had, if not a leader, at least a representative figure, and the orthodox public had a target. In Duret's words, the picture established between Manet and the public 'a complete alienation, an unending feud, which was to continue throughout the whole of his life'.

For years Manet filled this role. One of his pictures, 'Olympia', was accepted by the official Salon in 1865, and the fascinated crowds who flocked to abuse it were so violent that a special guard had to be put on duty near the painting. This was a period when the Salons were attracting the attention of a wider public than before, and Duret notes that the public at large showed itself

'more attached to convention and tradition, more hostile to novelty, less capable of correcting errors of judgement, than the limited world which had hitherto been the sole arbiter on matters of art'.

The opposition to Manet, he says, was more violent than to any previous innovator in French painting.

Early support for Manet and his fellow-rebels came neither from the public at large (from whom sentimental reformers often expect it) nor from the established sub-group of artists and professional art critics, but from a few people such as Baudelaire and Zola who were interested in art but not involved closely with the specialist sub-group. Zola's militant defence provoked so much opposition from the public that he had to be dropped by the paper for which he wrote. But it helped to sharpen the conflict still further, and to gather a group of militant disciples, mainly young painters, around Manet. Other innovations show the same feature: that early support comes neither from the community as a whole nor from the specialist sub-groups, but from a fringe of people between the two. For social plasticity the fringe of amateurs who can take an intelligent interest in a special line of work without being involved in its social and professional organisation is of the utmost importance. Beyond a certain point, increasing specialisation of function is a threat to plasticity, for it brings not only restrictions of knowledge and outlook but also an over-compact set of professional loyalties.

It is a commonplace that some part of the appeal of an innovation like Manet's lies in the mere fact of its being a revolt. Its early followers usually include, for instance, would-be innovators who want the attitudes and emotions that come with attacking the established order but who themselves have no significant new contribution to offer. Moreover, many of Manet's supporters gathered round him not only from direct admiration for his work, but also in reaction against the inordinate violence and bitterness of the public's opposition. Zola's own taste in painting was rather uncertain—as his letters to Cézanne show, it was at first highly traditional and based on literary sentiment—and his sympathy probably went as much to Manet the rebel and underdog as to Manet the painter. The adherents of a revolutionary movement may be strikingly different in spirit from the innovator himself.

From 1865 to 1881 the story is one of gradually widening sympathy for the Impressionists and for Manet who, though hardly a member of that school, could yet stand as a representative of their claim to the right of experiment and individual development. What seems to have happened is not that many members of the general public came to like Manet's work, but that the adherence to the innovating group of more and more otherwise respectable people produced in the general public slightly more deference, or at least less complacent contempt. What developed was not respect for the paintings but deference for a painter who was gaining reputable supporters. This again seems to be a very common social mechanism, one that crops up clearly in religious innovation and appears at its crudest when the conversion of a king brings a landslide of new believers. In less dramatic forms it occurs so often as to suggest that very few people pass a direct judgement on a proposed innovation: instead they assess it in terms of the social impression it already seems to be making.

Fluctuations of public and official favour continued during the years of gradual acceptance, Manet's pictures being sometimes accepted for the Salon, sometimes rejected. In 1873 the orthodox critics seized on what seemed to be a chance to put themselves in the right: Manet's picture in that year's Salon, 'Le Bon Bock', happened to represent a cheerful toper in a naturalistic style which everyone could understand. It became a popular favourite, the criitcs referred in a less hostile spirit to his earlier work, and the public felt sure that all they had previously objected to was the effect of youth. Manet, however, went on experimenting and his pictures for the next few years suffered varying fates at the hands of juries and critics. What the episode of 1873 showed was a readiness for tension to be reduced between the orthodox and the heretics and an increasing wish to assimilate the new movement to the acceptable tradition. After that, in spite of ups and downs, Manet's acceptance was certain, and in 1881 he received the medal of the Salon. His acceptance by the general public meant little more, of course, than toleration and, gradually, a claim to the bemused deference that any painter gains from having his work in the official galleries. But for those who were more actively concerned with painting it marked the influx of a new stream into the tradition of European painting.

Manet as a person was the focus of the social forces that first developed and then resolved the very strong tensions around this innovation. From one point of view his life history was an expression of those social forces. Equally, Manet was himself a potent social force, as any individual may be, and we need to look at the personal qualities which made him an innovator rather than a contributor to an innovating movement.

His great capacity as a painter was of course the first essential. After that there came the important and rare quality of taking his own experience seriously instead of filtering it through interpretations provided by society. For Manet it was visual experience that came freshly to him, but this is only a particular instance of the general quality which marks Trotter's 'sensitives'. To act as the focus of contemporary struggles Manet also needed another quality, his pugnacity. Only a combative man, such as he was, could have provided the hostile public with a responsive target and have made his fellow experimenters feel that he would serve as their spearhead if they gave him support. Finally—illustrating the point already mentioned—he was a sociable man to whom ordinary public liking and acclaim were intensely important.

The rareness of innovators is probably due in part to the need for this unusual combination of determined and even combative independence of mind with a strong, active need for approval and esteem. Manet was not an eccentric or a solitary nor the sort of bohemian who finds membership of a clique sufficient to compensate for the contempt or neglect of the ordinary public. He is said to have been a brilliant conversationalist and in manner a distinguished man of the world. He hated the derision and persecution to which he was subjected at first and he developed a touchiness about

it which became slightly paranoid. When in later life he was more
tolerated he still felt bitter, for one thing, because he made little
money and for another because he was regarded by the world at
large as inferior to some of his mediocre contemporaries. For him
the fact that he had influenced all the younger painters of any
importance and was surrounded by a circle of admirers was never
more than a consolation for being denied the wider acclaim that
he craved. With his eager hope for general appreciation he was unreasonably cheered by casual expressions of praise from a new
disciple or a friendly outsider, taking them to be the dawn of public
recognition. Far from pretending to despise the medal of the Salon
which had shown so little sympathy with his work he was un-
affectedly delighted, and called personally on each of the jurors who
had voted for him in order to offer his thanks.

The combination, superficially paradoxical, of a craving for the
affection and appreciation of one's group together with a life's work
that centres round combative antagonism to its standards is important enough in the psychology of innovation to be illustrated
further. It appears vividly in the personality of George Fox, the
founder of the Quakers, as he reveals it in the early pages of the
Journal.

Fox's extreme dissatisfaction with society and the perfunctory
religion of his time seems to go back to the fact that in later childhood he remained true to the ideals that he had absorbed from his
parents in his earliest years, although he naturally found that in
reality neither his parents nor other adults adhered to their own
precepts. For most children the discovery that grown-ups in their
own behaviour largely disregard their more pious instructions does
not precipitate a serious crisis; it may cause some distress but with
the help of rationalisation and conventional resistance to experience
most children fairly soon put the conflict beyond the reach of conscious concern. But Fox, for reasons about which we could now
only speculate, was extraordinarily meticulous in carrying out the
precepts he had been given.

'My father's name was Christopher Fox: he was by profession a weaver,
an honest man; and there was a seed of God in him. The neighbours called
him Righteous Christer. My mother was an upright woman; her maiden

name was Mary Lago, of the family of the Lagos, and of the stock of the martyrs.

'In my very young years I had a gravity and stayedness of mind and spirit, not usual in children; in so much, that when I saw old men carrying themselves lightly and wantonly towards each other, I had a dislike thereof raised in my heart, and said within myself, "If ever I come to be a man surely I shall not do so, nor be so wanton."

'When I came to eleven years of age, I knew pureness and righteousness; for while a child I was taught how to walk to be kept pure. The Lord taught me to be faithful in all things, and to act faithfully two ways, viz. inwardly to God, and outwardly to man; and to keep to Yea and Nay in all things.'

With this inconvenient determination to take the precepts of grown-ups literally and hold them to their word, Fox combined an unusual dependence on other people and what seems to have been an unusual shrinking from the conventional responsibilities of adulthood. He writes:

'When I was come down into Leicestershire, my relations would have had me marry, but I told them I was but a lad, and must get wisdom. Others would have had me into the Auxiliary Band among the soldiery but I refused; and I was grieved that they proffered such things to me, being a tender youth.'

This, at the age of twenty, and in the first half of the seventeenth century, suggests remarkable anxiety to remain in the shelter of immaturity.

Throughout the early pages of the *Journal* there is evidence of the severe conflict which Fox suffered between, on the one hand, his great dependence and strong desire for social sanction and approbation and, on the other, his acute realisation of the failure of society to live up to ideals which for him had the strongest social sanction of all: the word of God according to his parents' earliest teaching. The result was a sense of having been betrayed by the society which had given him his ideals, a sense of betrayal revealed vividly in an incident of his nineteenth year which seems to have been a turning-point in his life:

'When I came towards nineteen years of age, being upon business at a fair, one of my cousins whose name was Bradford, a professor, and having another professor with him, came to me and asked me to drink part of a jug of beer with them, and I, being thirsty, went in with them; for I loved any that had a sense of good, or that sought after the Lord. When we had drunk a glass apiece they began to drink healths, calling for more, and agreeing together that he that would not drink should pay all. I was grieved that any who made profession of religion should do so. They grieved me very much, having never had such a thing put to me before, by any sort of people; wherefore I rose up to be gone, and putting my hand into my pocket laid a groat on the table before them, and said, "If it be so, I'll leave you." So I went away; and when I had done what business I had to do, I returned home, but did not go to bed that night, nor could not sleep, but sometimes walked up and down, and sometimes prayed and cried to the Lord, who said unto me, "Thou seest how young people go together into vanity, and old people into the earth; thou must forsake all, both young and old, and keep out of all, and be as a stranger unto all." '

There then began a period of defensive isolation in which Fox left his relations 'and brake off all familiarity or fellowship with old or young'. This was to leave one horn of his dilemma for the other and, as one would expect, his conflict brought intense depression, feelings of guilt, and tendencies to remorse:

'Now during the time that I was at Barnet a strong temptation to despair came upon me. Then I saw how Christ was tempted, and mighty troubles I was in; sometimes I kept myself retired in my chamber, and often walked solitary in the Chace there, to wait upon the Lord. I wondered why these things should come to me; and I looked upon myself and said, "Was I ever so before?" Then I thought, because I had forsaken my relations I had done amiss against them; so I was brought to call to mind all the time that I had spent, and to consider whether I had wronged any. But temptations grew more and more and I was tempted almost to despair; and when Satan could not effect his design upon me that way, he laid snares for me and baits to draw me to commit some sin, whereby he might take advantage to bring me to despair. I was about twenty years of age when these exercises came upon me; and I continued in that condition some years, in great troubles, and fain I would have put it from me. I went to many a priest to look for comfort, but found no comfort from them.'

His conflict was thus between his desire to enjoy the sanction and support of a social group and the necessity to reject fiercely the only society he knew, since it violated his moral and religious standards. The solution to his dilemma came in the form of his 'openings from the Lord', or divine revelations, which began in his twenty-second year. These openings seem to have been ideas that occurred to him in the ordinary way except that they carried such extraordinary conviction that Fox was never in any doubt of their having divine sanction. The ideas in themselves were not extraordinary, but they were subversive of the orthodox views of the people Fox was living among and he could have got no ordinary social sanction for them. His curious dependence on others (in spite of his obstinate holding out against them) made it necessary for him to have some more than personal support for personal opinions that challenged society and its orthodoxies. The second of the openings he records shows well the sort of function they fulfilled for him:

'At another time, as I was walking in a field on a First-day morning, the Lord opened to me that being bred at Oxford or Cambridge was not enough to fit and qualify men to be ministers of Christ; and I stranged at it because it was the common belief of people. But I saw it clearly as the Lord opened it to me, and was satisfied, and admired the goodness of the Lord who had opened this thing unto me that morning.'

To point out the social needs for which a religious conviction may serve as a substitute satisfaction has, of course, no theological significance. It says nothing one way or the other about the divine origin or the divine sanction of, say, Fox's revelations. Psychologically, however, it is important to see the significance these revelations had as a means of satisfying social needs that were otherwise frustrated. Not only did they give him the necessary sanction for believing fully and boldly in his reforming opinions, they also gave him the consolation of feeling that someone understood him, sympathised with him and could help him.

After his revelations had begun, his conflict was largely ended. He indicates the vital point after describing how he went unprofitably from sect to sect but finally left them all,

'for I saw there was none among them all that could speak to my condition. And when all my hopes in them and in all men were gone, so that I had nothing outwardly to help me, nor could I tell what to do; then, oh! then I heard a voice which said, "There is one, even Christ Jesus, that can speak to thy condition": and when I heard it, my heart did leap for joy. Then the Lord did let me see why there was none upon the earth that could speak to my condition, namely, that I might give Him all the glory. . . .'

In other words, the elements of the previous conflict now showed themselves to him as features of a divine pattern, and from this point Fox went on towards the supreme confidence in himself that marked his later character.

The subtle balance in some innovators between strong opposition to contemporary group standards and strong need of social approbation is brought out by a contrasting type of innovator. Cézanne's personality had several strong resemblances to Manet's but was yet so different essentially that it might seem to be almost an accident that he had influence as an innovator at all. The history of his work also illustrates a different set of social processes from those previously mentioned earlier as a common pattern of social innovation.

It appears from the account given by Mack (1935) that in his young days Cézanne showed some traits that might have been expected to produce a public combatant like Manet. He was outspokenly contemptuous and hostile towards the orthodox painting of the day. He was capable of truculence, not to say arrogance. In 1866 when the Salon rejected his pictures, he wrote to the Superintendent of the École des Beaux Arts protesting against the rejection and demanding another Salon des Refusés even if his pictures were the only ones exhibited in it. And in this letter, speaking of the jury's decision, he writes:

'I shall content myself with saying once more that I cannot accept the unfair judgement of colleagues to whom I myself have not given the authority to appraise me'

—a piece of quite infantile arrogance since it was he who chose to submit his pictures. This demand for approbation exclusively on one's own terms suggests the immature attitude which wants the social world to be simply a mirror reflecting and intensifying the glory one already sees in oneself. It is not by any means self-sufficiency, for the desire to have one's excellence mirrored remains very strong in such a man and (as will appear) Cézanne had a deep craving for recognition and esteem.

More superficially too his social make-up was very different from Manet's. For a few years he was an occasional member of the group attached to Manet who met at the Café Guerbois, but he is said to have been awkward and unpolished, ill at ease in company, and prone to explosive outbursts of rage if he let himself get involved in argument. He had had temper tantrums as a child and never got over a liability to violent outbursts of anger for seemingly trivial causes. He had very few friends and was generally uneasy at the possibility of any relation that would give other people claims upon him. He saw all attachments as *grappins*—grappling irons—and evidently viewed people as potential interferers rather than as potential friends and supporters.

When he met with thwarting his most natural response seems to have been withdrawal. Passive resistance, patient persistence and some deceit were the means he used to overcome his domineering father's opposition first to his career as a painter and later to his marriage. Hostility without combat was his method. After repeated rejections by the Salon he exhibited twice (in 1874 and in 1877) with the Impressionist group in private galleries and was treated with contempt by the public and almost all the critics, including even one who was tepidly favourable to other members of the group. After that, he withdrew into almost complete isolation and no longer exhibited with the Impressionists, though they would have been glad to have his work. He still wanted the official acceptance of the Salon and continued for many years to submit his pictures, only to have them regularly rejected by the juries. On two occasions, by what amounted to tricks, he got a picture into official exhibitions, once the Salon and once an international exhibition, and on both occasions he was totally ignored. Otherwise between 1877 and 1890 there was no public exhibition of his work. Dealers and collectors, critics and even painters (apart from a few friends such as Pissarro, Renoir and Monet) knew nothing of his work and virtually forgot his existence. It seems characteristic that when the 'authoritative' judges rejected his work he did not attach himself effectively to the militant innovating group among whom he would have been just one respected member. Instead he withdrew to a solitary life in which he set about with incredible persistence the endless study and development of his individual line of work in painting. Ethically the case illustrates that uncertain borderline where rather morbid self-centredness shades into single-minded devotion to one's own proper functioning and loyalty to the development of one's unique talent. Socially the fascinating problem is how to distinguish between a valuable persistence in individual development and the stubbornness of worthless self-conceit.

If we inquire what led to Cézanne's defiance we have to suppose that in large measure his rebellion against authority and orthodox views in painting was a continuation of the rebellion against his father's authority that took him into painting at all. His early work gives little or no indication of the kind and quality of the work he did later, and it looks as if dissatisfaction and rebellion came first, long before a convincing alternative to orthodoxy had been glimpsed. The same is probably true of many innovators. It adds to the understandable difficulties of orthodox contemporaries since at first they see little except the negative rebellion and are amply furnished with rationalisations for their inertia.

Cézanne's secret evaluation of himself was extraordinarily high. It was so high and in effect so belittling of others that both prudence and secret guilt led him to conceal it in outward humility and isolation and even to refuse suspiciously the occasional expressions of admiration that he was offered. Mack's account of Cézanne's early relations with Joachim Gasquet illustrates this side of his personality. Gasquet was one of the young men who towards the end of Cézanne's life discovered and valued his work, and whose admiring friendship mitigated his isolation. Gasquet's first expression of enthusiastic admiration was met with Cézanne's usual suspicion —he rounded on the young man for making fun of him—but after a few minutes he accepted Gasquet's sincerity and became warmly responsive to him. They saw each other constantly for about a week. To quote Gasquet's words,

'All his self-confidence came back to him. At last he began to talk about his own genius. One evening, he let himself go and declared: "I am the only living painter!" Then he clenched his fists, relapsed into gloomy silence. He went home grimly as if some disaster had overtaken him.'

Gasquet was right. Psychologically, a disaster had happened: he had let the cat out of the bag with a vengeance and was, of course, assailed with guilt and anxiety at having made such a claim. Possibly he had never before made it consciously even to himself.

The result was that he cut himself off from Gasquet for several days, refusing to see him when he called. Then he met Gasquet and Mme Gasquet out for a walk. Gasquet saluted him but Cézanne trudged on pretending not to see them. Next day Gasquet got a letter in which Cézanne said that he had seen them but that Gasquet had appeared to be very angry with him—a projective attribution to Gasquet of the anger he felt against himself. He then went on with a letter of self-exculpation in which, without mentioning his boastful claim, he puts the blame for it on the people who, towards the end of his life, had begun to praise his work in public. Their praise had been quite moderate but it looks as though Cézanne unconsciously viewed any praise as the first indulgence of an inordinate and insatiable appetite for esteem, an invitation to betray himself into what, sanely, he knew to be an overweening self-conceit that would simply sweep away and annihilate all his colleagues and rivals. He said in this letter:

'If you could see my real self, my inner man, you would not be angry. Don't you see after all to what a sad state I am reduced? Not master of myself, a man who does not exist, and you try to be a philosopher who in the end will annihilate me altogether. But I curse the ——s and the clowns who have drawn the attention of the public to me in order to sell their fifty-franc articles. All my life I have worked in the hope of being able to earn a living, but I thought it would be possible to paint well without drawing attention to my private affairs. Certainly an artist wants to reach the highest possible intellectual heights, but the man should remain in obscurity. The joy should be in the work.'

A similar mechanism was at work in an earlier incident, recorded by Mack, when a few Impressionist painters, friends and acquaintances of his, gave a small luncheon party in his honour.

F

'When Cézanne arrived the others were already gathered around the table, and Monet began a little speech of welcome in which he expressed the deep admiration and affection that all of those present felt for their colleague. Cézanne listened with his head bowed and his eyes full of tears; and when Monet had finished he said: "Ah, Monet, even you make fun of me!" To the consternation of everyone, and in spite of all protests, he rushed from the room. He did not come back, nor could he ever be convinced that the homage of the other painters had been sincere.'

With this degree of insecurity and *malaise* in his social life it is not surprising that Cézanne's working life was exceptionally isolated even in comparison with the lives of others who have original work to do. The interesting inquiry is how far there was *any* effective contact between him and his social group and by what social process his work came eventually to be assimilated into the tradition of painting.

It is clear to begin with that he was greatly helped in his early working life by discovering the small sub-group of innovators associated with Manet and the Salon des Refusés of 1863. Previously he had been in rebellion against the academic tradition but had had no positive direction; to quote Mack,

'He felt that he knew what was wrong with the teachings of the academicians, but he did not yet know how to set them right. He was still floundering, and, as far as he knew, he was floundering alone.'

The group who later became the Impressionists, though they helped Cézanne, gave him only a very general working direction. He never conformed to them, nor, as he came to define himself more exactly, did he try to influence their work. During the most important part of his life he seems to have achieved unselfconscious absorption in his task and to have been very little distracted or divided by concern for its social effect. Society's links with his work were extremely tenuous; in the main they consisted of Tanguy, the colour merchant who took Cézanne's paintings in settlement of bills for colours and stored them in his shop, one or two painters who remembered and respected his work, and a civil servant who was an enthusiastic admirer and bought some of the pictures. Yet towards the end of his life there came a relatively sudden wave of appreciation for him from young painters and critics who had grown up in the atmosphere of Impressionism and were now ready for developments beyond it. Cézanne's case illustrates the possibility that a sub-group may unwittingly be preparing itself to adopt new practices and interests of which consciously it knows practically nothing. His innovation was complete before any sub-group formed around it.

It seems almost an accident that Cézanne was regarded as an innovator in his own lifetime. He dealt differently with the social cravings that compelled Manet and Fox, for instance, to insist pugnaciously on recognition for their work; helped no doubt by the psychopathology that showed him all social relations as *grappins*, he rejected the rejecting social group. In slightly different circumstances he might well have been one of those who do original work which comes to be valued only many years after their deaths. Mendel's work on biological inheritance, for instance, published in 1866, was ignored until the facts had been independently re-discovered in 1900. He too, for different reasons from Cézanne, had no need to fight for social recognition of his work. Whether the contributions of these less combatant innovators are assimilated by their contemporary social group or ignored and wasted will depend on facts of social organisation and the psychological climate of a period that could be illuminated only by a closer analysis than social psychology has so far attempted.

13

THE AVERAGE AND THE EXCELLENT

Difficulties encountered in several spheres of social life, those connected with competition, leadership, occupational prestige, innovation, to mention a few, are often peripheral effects of a more central problem. This problem, not yet studied systematically by psychology, is the relation between abler people and the less able, particularly the relation between the average and those who are better than average in some direction. The problem is one that societies have always had to face and have probably never more than partially solved. One attempted solution has been seen in social orders that try to maintain a 'station in life' for everyone and put barriers in the way of his leaving it. Religious teaching associated with such an order in the Middle Ages set itself firmly against envy and covetousness, regarding emulation as something to be encouraged, if at all, only in very limited spheres. An index of our own society's difficulty in dealing with the question is seen in the history of words like envy, jealousy and emulation. The Oxford English Dictionary shows that we have never managed to fix linguistically the concept of generous admiration for good fortune or achievement that goes beyond our own; any word used for this purpose seems at some point in its history to convey the sense of a grudge or ill-will against the superiority of others.

'Emulation', with its sense of active effort to reach or outdo others, is at present fairly respectable, though for different reasons it is losing the value it had in the nineteenth century. Then the full acceptance of competition in the economic sphere led to an emphasis on emulation in all directions as a moral duty. There was a lamentable tendency to see worldly success as a sign of moral rectitude and hence to make the lack of it a personal and moral disparagement; and this attitude retained plenty of life until the unemployment experiences of the nineteen-thirties. There is truth, of course, in the view that some of the ordinary moral virtues contribute to material success, but so many other factors intervene that a belief in a perfect correlation between virtue and prosperity is one-sided. Unfortunately it leads to an equally one-sided reaction against giving people any credit for outstanding achievement or any encouragement to surpass others in any direction. This is unfortunate for the interests of the group, for it seems likely that social progress of all kinds occurs through the consolidation of salients rather than through a simultaneous advance on the whole front.

The development of individual capacities beyond what is usual in any direction brings the need for some consequent social adjustment between the exceptional individual and his average companions in the community or his special sub-group. One of the psychological merits of games and amateur sports has been that they provide an area where the relation of the able to the less able has been institutionalised in a way that people at all levels of ability feel to be fair, in which standards are objectively established, and in which even the less able enjoy the satisfactions that are commensurate with their achievement. One need not idealise this field of activity or overlook its limitations, but in comparison with other areas of social life it shows striking success in dealing with the problems of standards of achievement and recognition of superiority.

In economic and professional life, money and positions of power give a fairly objective index of one aspect of 'success', but even for those who regard this as equivalent to success without inverted commas the position is complicated by the great contribution to 'success' that may be made by dishonesty, self-publicity, flattery, nepotism and similar factors. Reasons are only too easily found for withholding whole-hearted respect from those who have got ahead of you in worldly ways; at the worst you can invoke 'luck' to explain it away.

Similar problems are still more difficult in the field of literature and the arts where no objective standard for distinguishing between the good and the better can be demonstrated and where a particularly unhealthy relation, involving contempt and resentment, may grow up between highbrows and lowbrows. Evasions of the problem are familiar in attempts to deny that there can be any greater or lesser achievement: 'it's all a matter of taste', 'they're equally good of their kind', 'it depends on your mood', and so forth. Some easing of the tension is found in a device that is also a favourite in dealing with the spiritually or morally outstanding, that of setting them on a pedestal well out of the way. Great figures are put *hors concours* and given an eminence that leaves them irrelevant to any of the standards of everyday life. Not the least unfortunate result of this device is the way that it leaves the spurious high-brow to flourish undisturbed by sharing the insulation of the great. A vivid example of this device is to be found in a letter to the London *Evening Standard* of 25th January, 1951:

' "Londoner's Diary" does well to draw attention to Lord Reith's vigorous denunciation of the B.B.C. "Third Programme". Millions will agree with him that Sophocles, Shakespeare, Shaw, Thomas Mann, Bach, Beethoven, Benjamin Britten, Alban Berg, Lord Rutherford, Cockcroft, Coulson, Gilbert Murray, T. S. Eliot, Dylan Thomas, etc. are all very well in their proper place. Let us, for goodness' sake, keep them there!'

The broad problem is that of a social group's use of its human wealth: whether as average people, who largely control the affairs of our group, we can make the best of those who excel us. The question is met early in life, in the handling of the exceptional child by parents and teachers. Here at once we are struck with the vast amount of psychological knowledge, advice and trained personnel that are available for aiding the mentally or physically handicapped child compared with the meagreness of the interest taken in the exceptionally able. For one thing, there is no doubt that in our culture most people's sentiments are organised in a way that makes it easier to lavish attention on the unfortunate than to help the gifted to make the most of themselves. Either effort requires great emotional discipline—the gifted and the wretched are both very trying—but our culture gives more encouragement to the effort towards helping the unfortunate.

It is illuminating, for instance, to observe how little space is given in text-books of educational psychology to advising teachers in training on the special difficulties that may arise from the fact that a sizable minority of the children they teach will be more intelligent than themselves. Knight (1933) reports the proportion of graduates at one of the British universities over an unstated 'period of years' who reached various levels of performance at intelligence tests: those with an I.Q. of over 100 amounted to 76 per cent, compared with 50 per cent in the population at large; those with an I.Q. of over 110 amounted to 42 per cent, compared with 20 to 25 per cent in the population at large. To put these figures the other way on, 58 per cent had an I.Q. of not more than 110; a large proportion of such graduates become teachers; and if their classes are a random sample of the population, these teachers will be faced with children of whom 20 to 25 per cent have a higher I.Q. than themselves. The precise figures may be wrong and universities may differ to some extent, but the broad conclusion is sound enough. For some considerable proportion of teachers, moreover, not only will an appreciable number of young pupils be of higher I.Q. (i.e. abler, as judged by the tests, in relation to others of their age) but a number of the adolescent pupils will actually have a higher mental age than their teacher.

The figures only confirm the common-sense expectation that teachers must often have to deal with pupils who are potentially abler than themselves, and in doing so they have, of course, the advantages of greater information, more experienced judgement, special training and skills, and various useful habits of mind. There is no reason why the exceptional child should not look back in later life gratefully and with respect to a teacher of only average ability. In fact at all ages it is a tribute to good functional leadership if an outstanding subordinate can think with respect and liking of a former leader whose achievement he has himself outstripped. Too often, however, the able child develops antipathy or apathy towards many of his teachers. Neither he nor they may know why, but the trouble is commonly connected with their failure to elicit what he is capable of and to expect the right things of him; if they give him the treatment that his companions want—and that they themselves wanted at his age—they will be failing him.

It seems on the face of it far from certain that the teacher's advantage in acquired abilities and perhaps in mental age will automatically show him how to handle a mind of better quality than his own. This would remain a doubt even if we were talking only of the rather simple differences in mental efficiency that the tests measure. If we consider subtler differences in the quality of minds, such as their relative capacity for bringing inchoate affective states into manageable cognitive terms without impoverishing them, or their tendency to seek out new questions rather than supply answers to ready-made problems, then it becomes still more unlikely that an average mind will be able to understand and help in the development of an exceptional mind without a considerable discipline of self-effacement and of tentativeness in the help proffered. It is never certain that the mature average mind will even notice the exceptional quality of an immature mind. Very little psychological inquiry has been directed towards qualitative differences in mental functioning of the kind that the intelligence tests may neglect in their quantitative measurements. A small beginning has been made in the experimental work on individual differences in 'rigidity' (cf. Chown, 1959) and 'creativeness' (cf. Taylor, 1956), but it will be long before these subtler aspects of intelligence have been fully explored and their relevance to the relations between average and exceptional minds brought out.

It is at any rate evident that unless the parents can provide it themselves, a gifted child's first contact with adult minds of average capacity is likely to come through some of his teachers. The sort of relations then established, whether of trust and mutual respect or of frustration and suspicion, may go far towards deciding whether anything like the full value of the gifted mind, to itself and to the average people of its social group, will be developed.

Problems of this kind have been very little investigated. Psychologists have to a remarkable extent concentrated their studies on those who are in one way or another of lower status than themselves in some hierarchy. Their widespread reliance on students as subjects for the study of personality has been commented on by more than one critic, and this is only part of a broader tendency. The bulk of the psychological investigation of human beings has concerned itself with children, students, the lower ranks of industry and the fighting services, neurotics, psychotics and other handicapped people, delinquents and 'primitive' peoples. There are all sorts of reasons for this, some of them good; and undoubtedly a great deal of general significance can be discovered from such studies. But it remains a limitation that psychologists have been able to give so little direct attention to those more distinguished than themselves and to the qualities that make for excellence in civilised directions. On the whole, though with some important exceptions, the littleness of the great has drawn more psychological attention than their greatness.

Surprisingly little is known about the processes involved in the individual's development towards what he believes to be a higher standard in some direction, and further information about these processes would be needed if we were to understand more fully the social relations between people whose standards of achievement differ. The following simple statement reported in a newspaper conceals exceedingly difficult unsolved problems; it refers to Mr. Tyrone Guthrie's tour of Australia to advise on the development of a national theatre there:

'In Mr. Guthrie's view neither Australian amateurs nor Australian audiences had sufficent sense of standards to detect the first-rate from the second-rate, since they had little opportunity of developing such standards. Mr. Guthrie recommended the systematic importation from the United Kingdom of first quality theatrical companies' (London *Times*, 19th April, 1949).

Among the questions raised by this passage is that of the relation between on the one hand, detecting successfully what the experts say is good, and, on the other hand, coming to like it oneself. One remembers, for instance, Margaret Bulley's (1952) inquiries into children's ability to distinguish the first-rate in pictures from the second-rate, and one well-trained child's remark that he could always make the right choice because he chose the picture

G

he didn't like and said that was 'art'. We also need to know what one thinks about one's own earlier preferences after advancing to more satisfying standards, and whether the process is irreversible or whether regressions to earlier preferences occur. And these are only a few of the unsolved problems raised by the seemingly simple and certainly very familiar matter of changing standards and preferences.

Again, when changes of standard occur in a social setting they are affected by what we know of other people's standards, or what we think we know, and by our attitude to those other people. Little is known psychologically about the impressions we have of other people's standards and our possible misunderstandings of them. Adverse criticism of our own preferences by other people is another familiar feature of everyday life, especially for the young, but we can go little beyond surmise in saying what characteristics of the critic, of the criticism, of the person criticised, and of the topic and circumstances, make for a positive and constructive response to criticism. Again, by what processes do we come to form our ambitions and what feelings develop in us towards those who seem to us, or are thought by others, to have outdistanced us in some desirable direction? We know very little with any certainty about the factors leading towards generous admiration of superior achievement instead of jealousy and resentment. Nor can we say in what circumstances the benefits of admiration and the stimulus to reasonable ambition become lost in the more futile developments of hero-worship.

One popular line of investigation in modern psychology which might seem to promise information on some of these points is concerned with 'level of aspiration'. But the experimental attack on the topic has consisted rather disappointingly in getting the subject (usually a student or a mental patient) to perform some little laboratory task, such as dart-throwing, and after he has seen the result of his attempt at the task to tell the experimenter and perhaps other onlookers how well he expects to do at the next attempt. The results of these experiments, dubious of interpretation in detail, suggest broadly that the subject's behaviour in this social situation is affected by various personality traits and neurotic tendencies. The contrast between the impressive label, 'level of aspiration', with its rich suggestion of social relevance, and the niggling reality is un-happily characteristic of much experimental work in social psycho-logy at the present time. No one would deny that such laboratory work might in time, especially if we can become clearer about what the subject is really doing when he announces his 'aspiration', develop into something of value. Up to now there has been little progress towards bridging the gap between this work and matters of concern to educated people.

It is the alert layman who in the end can do as much as anyone to influence, by the questions he asks, the growth of a branch of science like social psychology. Questions about the relation between those of higher and those of lower ability and achievement are well worth asking at the present time on account of the fruitful perplexity in which we stand. In Victorian times it would have seemed superfluous and impious to question the programme of whole-hearted emulation, with easy-minded enjoyment of your rewards, material and psychological, or with humble recognition of your failure. In understandable reaction against that programme, and the complacency it engendered in the successful, we have been through a period in which low standards of achievement, material and moral, tended perhaps too readily to be explained as a result of undeserved misfortune in one's early economic or psychological circumstances. There has perhaps been some tendency to evade the social problems that result from the differences between people in their abilities, achievements and standards of behaviour. The whole question has recently been too much complicated by political cleavages to encourage detached psychological discussion, but it seems likely that people of varying political leanings now recognise more readily that there is in this area of human relations an unsolved social problem.

In its commonest everyday aspects the problem appears in terms of occupational achievement and moral behaviour. But this is a section of the wider topic of standards of achievement in general (including range and sensitivity of interest and the disciplined development of values in any direction) and the effects on social relations of differences in these respects between one person and another. It is an aspect of social life which has been a recurrent concern of people who are capable of seeing it.

There are plenty of emotive expressions of opinion one way and the other. On the one hand, there is the popular and hopeful view that we needs must love the highest when we see it. On the other, we have for instance the reflection that Jane Austen expresses through Emma when she contemplates Mr. Elton's presumptuousness:

'Perhaps it was not fair to expect him to feel how very much he was her inferior in talent, and all the elegancies of mind. The very want of such equality might prevent his perception of it.'

And Blake is more positive:

'Is not Merit in one a Cause of Envy in another, and Serenity and Happiness and Beauty a Cause of Malevolence?' (quoted by Wilson, 1927).

Yet there are also such experiences as that of Edward FitzGerald on a visit to Tennyson:

'I will say no more of Tennyson than that the more I have seen of him, the more cause I have to think him great. . . . I felt what Charles Lamb describes, a sense of depression at times from the overshadowing of so much more lofty intellect than my own: this (though it may seem vain to say so) I never experienced before, though I have often been with much greater intellects: but I could not be mistaken in the universality of his mind; and perhaps I have received some benefit in the now more distinct consciousness of my dwarfishness' (quoted by Terhune, 1947).

These are varied responses to the recognition of differences of merit between one person and another. To rest content with the truism that they reflect 'individual differences' would be scientifically indolent. We need far more knowledge of the qualities of mind and the features of circumstance that make for this or that kind of response.

Harmony and stability in a social group, and the possibility of maximum creative achievement, depend partly on the existence of a healthy relation between the able and the less able in the various directions of human effort. The fact that in most directions most of us are average, taken together with the fact that we like esteem and prestige, has seemed to some psychologists to constitute a dilemma. Lasswell (1935) seems to imply that the pressure to gain distinction is so great that everyone's happiness demands his feeling that he is at the top of a pyramid at least in some detail of activity. Even if this could be arranged it would be a precarious condition of happiness. We may to some extent have been led astray by the Adlerian emphasis on a striving for superiority as the outcome of one's awareness of helplessness in infancy. There seems no good reason why the young should crave achievement far beyond their capacity; the young of other animals appear not to; and if the human young do, that would appear to be a culturally induced trait. It may well be that the competitive tendencies of western culture have here exacerbated a problem that could be less serious. A team of American psychologists (Child, *et al.*, 1946) has analysed the themes met with in American stories for children, pointing to their heavy emphasis on the importance of 'success' as a condition of happiness and commenting on the contrast between the great self-expectations thus inculcated in children and the small possibilities of such success in their adult world.

Emphasis on a rather abstract, theoretical notion of 'success' no doubt does cause some unnecessary mental discomfort to the average person who cannot shine, but in practical reality the difficulty seems exaggerated. It seems likely that what most people want is not, as Lasswell implies, to be at the top of a pyramid of deference but to have recognition for their abilities and merits at whatever point in the pyramid they may have reached. Naturally they like to be reminded most often of the ways in which they excel large numbers of other people (as we nearly all do in one direction or another) and not to have to think too frequently of those who excel them. But so long as their real worth is given ungrudging recognition most people are reasonably satisfied. They may wish for higher status in some direction, and perhaps strive for it, but they are not doomed to unhappiness if they fail to reach preeminence. Why should average people not be happy in a culture like ours? The Press, the political parties, entertainment, sport, organised religion, industrial design and the dress trade all cater mainly for them; the fiction shelves of circulating libraries are packed with books that appeal to them, they can open a mass-circulation newspaper almost anywhere and find it interesting, and they can view the television for long periods with enjoyment.

As average people we owe our comparatively high standard of living—comparatively high both materially and in such matters as kindness, humanity, toleration, literacy and freedom from the grosser superstitions—to the salients thrust out in various directions by unusual people. The problems and difficulties met with by those people, whether the pre-eminent innovators or those who make the smaller explorations and advances, are not the concern merely of the exceptional people themselves; they concern the rest of us, who may as a group be wasting our resources by giving too little help to people better than ourselves. So too the average person's difficulties in adjusting himself to the claims and challenges of those who outshine him might profitably be considered with more sympathy and understanding by those of superior ability or unusual development.

How we can hope to discriminate between the potential innovator and the crank, how we can save the exceptionally able person from superciliousness and self-conceit and spare the average the wasteful experiences of jealousy and resentment, how we can face the prospect of changing our beliefs and practices without needless anxiety, and how we can combine both stability and plasticity in our group life, are questions that intelligent laymen might well ask social psychology to consider more closely.

Faced with these psychological problems we may be inclined to turn aside into ethics, aesthetics, social philosophy and political science. For social psychologists this is a temptation to be resisted, however valid an undertaking for those with the appropriate interests and qualifications. The target for us is the large psychological element in the questions; our concern is with the *psychological* processes associated with choices and evaluations. Whether they involve value 'judgements' may be left to philosophers to dispute and, we may hope, decide. The intelligent layman who is concerned with these issues in a practical way can legitimately hope that a great deal more purely psychological information will in time be available about them. We shall become increasingly aware of the need for this information as we give more attention to the question of 'social advance', when that phrase is taken to mean, not merely the elevation of the less fortunate to our own level, but a development that may demand changes in ourselves, with the recognition of excellence that we cannot achieve and even a belief that there may be excellences the possibility of which we have not yet managed to notice. If we are ever to glimpse them it will depend on the use that our social group can make of individuals who excel us and who are not always the most comfortable people to know.

14

RESTATEMENT

The theme of this book has been the development of the social individual, the being who could realise virtually none of his possibilities without the elicitations offered by a social group, but whose growth remains individual, sometimes falling short of what his society expects, sometimes going beyond it, sometimes taking directions that no member of the group has previously explored. Equally the subject matter can be seen as the conditions and processes affecting a social group's use of its human resources, particularly its problem of maintaining enough conformity to its standards for continuity and stability, while permitting enough individual divergences to ensure plasticity and give it opportunities of glimpsing its limitations and reconsidering its assumptions.

The view has been argued that man is naturally a social animal, in the same sense as we can say that he is naturally a food-seeking animal or naturally a sexual animal; we need not suppose that his social impulses are derived indirectly from some other part of his psychological constitution or that participation in social life is something thrust upon him, a trick that a solitary animal has reluctantly learned to perform. At the same time social responsiveness, like almost all men's capacities, has to be socially elicited; without human contact in early life it would hardly exist, and with the wrong sort of human contact in the earliest days it may remain rudimentary, as in the so-called affectionless characters and the 'psychopathic personality' type (whose defect may indeed be con-

stitutional). The difference between them and the rest of us helps
to emphasise the ready spontaneity with which social responsiveness and an inclination to value human companionship for its own
sake emerge in most human beings.

It would, however, be a mistake to suppose that because men
are sociable they put friendly companionship with their fellows
above all other goods. The fact is that our social impulses and the
sentiments in which they are organised are only part of our total
system of values and may easily conflict with other impulses and
desires; our human companions often become obstacles to the ful-
filment of other important desires. Obstacles to our desires naturally
arouse pugnacity and fellow-beings, therefore, become at times the
object of attack. But an attack on people to whom we are attached
sets up conflict and remorse; and with the strengthening of social
sentiments, and the extension (partly through reasoning) of the
range of men and women to whom they apply, many people
reach the point where an attack on any human being is repugnant.
The actual killing of others, the final aggression, may come to
seem unjustifiable in any circumstances. Yet to act on this conviction would at times involve the sacrifice of other very highly
important values; and this is the central dilemma of communities
that have far-extended social values but exist in an international
framework that retains war as one of its institutions.

War is not a thing *sui generis* but an intensification of the rivalry,
aggression and hatred which run all though our social intercourse
and the control of which has been one of the objects of child-rearing
and law-enforcement throughout history. One of the chief contributions of psycho-analysis has been the demonstation that hostility
generated by all sorts of frustrations is easily pent up within us,
without our being more than very imperfectly aware of it, and is
readily displaced on to other objects than those by which it was set
up. It is this fact that offers a hope of diminishing the quarrelsomeness of human beings, both by minimising their frustrations and
by reaching better techniques for dealing with the pugnacity that
inevitable frustrations will arouse.

The fact that the human species is both sociable and pugnacious
is one of the complexities that rule out simple ideals and simple

remedies in the field of human relations. One of the most angering frustrations, for instance, is the frustration of anger; and the attempt to live in the fantasy that human beings could be all loving kindness produces dangerous accumulations of repressed rage. Too much of our moral effort has followed the pattern represented by parents who tell a child that it's wicked to hate his little brother and—even more fantastic—that it's wicked to hate them; instead of helping him to accept less uncomfortably the fact that he will inevitably hate them all, sometimes, as well as loving them much of the time.

Much frustration, however, that seems at first sight inevitable arises from the fact that our civilisation has institutionalised recourse to the relation of domination and submission (or attempted domination and resistance) as the usual way of handling a conflict of aim between two people. It never has been the only way of dealing with such a conflict, and psychological work during the last thirty years has made much clearer the nature and conditions of the 'integrative' handling of conflict. Developments in industry and in child psychology especially have given hints of the greatly extended range of situations in which integrative behaviour could become usual. Psychotherapy has illuminated the conditions making for the psychological security without which integrative behaviour is impossible. This is a point at which psychological studies have allowed us to see an overlooked cultural assumption—a social institution disguised as 'human nature'—which is responsible for some of the most severe of our self-created difficulties.

The development of the child's social responsiveness, a process that has received fairly close psychological study, implies the need to reach a balance between attachment to others and potential hostility against them in some of their aspects. The possibility of meeting this difficult challenge depends on the mutual willingness of mother and child to tolerate a gradual diminution in the intensity of the early sentiment uniting them and to gain part of their sense of social welcome (and the psychological security that it brings) from contacts with other people. For the child this means amongst other things discovering the importance of his coevals as companions and not just as rivals for the affectionate attention of adults; and this, as Piaget has shown, has important consequences for the individual's later morality, since it involves a gradual acceptance of coevals as a source of social sanction and authority in place of earlier dependence for moral guidance upon parents, parent-surrogates such as teachers and clergy, or parent-lieutenants such as older siblings. Much moral development and much of what is sometimes called 'emotional maturity' are aspects of the gradually unfolded implications of our social nature.

One feature of social life is the opportunities it gives of measuring our achievement against others, being stimulated by the challenge of theirs and experiencing the satisfaction of giving and receiving esteem. This is the satisfactory aspect of competition, and in various forms of friendly competition it produces no difficulty. Difficulties arise, however, in serious competition (for instance, for goods in short supply) where the success of one person brings deprivation to another; and also in a society such as ours where competitiveness as a trait of personality can come to have a compulsive and irrational quality. Different cultures and different periods have handled the problem of competition in diverse ways, ranging from institutions that make competition for many sorts of goods pointless, through codes of fair play and generosity towards losers, to the sanctioning of ruthless competition as a positively moral way of life. The variety of methods for dealing with the problem, each with its disadvantages, suggests that in this area of human relations social learning still has far to go.

Competition for material goods is the simplest part of the problem. Competition for prestige and social respect is more complex; and it remains no less important a part of our social life because of the decay of the older class system in which it was partly expressed and partly controlled. There has been for some time a general trend in our culture for the individual's personal qualities to count more, and his membership of a social class or other group to count less, in securing him esteem. Individuals are tending to matter more than categories. But many social groupings, especially occupational, still contribute largely to the social prestige of their members. It is one of the tasks of social psychology to identify the gradients of respect which contribute jointly and confusedly to the general esteem in which the various occupations are held. The topic is of importance to the general theme of this book because the qualities that help to confer social status give a broad indication of the society's prevailing values. Though one class system after another may decay there is no reason to expect the disappearance of roughly defined sub-divisions within society which are held in different degrees of esteem and confer status on their members.

There is equally no likelihood of the emergence of any social order which would fail to recognise the relation of leader to subordinate for functional purposes when people join together in certain kinds of tasks. Differences of skill, experience and judgement, and the convenience of having someone to share out work amongst a team and take responsibility when rapid decisions are imperative, all help to give the leader functions that make him welcome to his functional subordinates. What is nowadays less welcome is the tendency for leadership in a particular function to be generalised, so that the leader is given deference in areas of social contact far beyond the sphere in which it is his function to lead. In the past this tendency caused people first to think of leadership in terms of 'superior and subordinate' and then, if they were not careful, to slide imperceptibly from that into 'superior and inferior'. That usage (with the outlook it implied) is now moribund, though still not dead. Much more effort is being made to understand and to bear in mind the fact of personal equality between those who occupy a different status in relation to a particular job. And while psychological measurement has rightly occupied itself with the inequalities between people in terms of any particular function, psychological thinking has perhaps been too little concerned in examining the implications of a notion of personal equality which is compatible with individual differences of ability and function.

It would, of course, be an impossibly simple society in which everyone competed for the same sort of goods, secured esteem for the same reasons, and led or followed in the same directions. A psychological account of any actual community must be an account of its sub-groups, based on occupation, recreation, geographical region, political outlook, religion, age, sex and a host of other interests and characteristics. All of them stand for different developments of function and different values in one direction or another, though in certain essentials they accept the dominant value system of the main community. The sub-groups range in size and clarity of definition from a single family, through a religion or profession, to a vaguely defined social 'class' or an amorphous body of people such as 'the elderly'. They overlap intricately with each other, and each individual belongs simultaneously to a very large number of them. It is they which have helped to elicit his more specialised interests and which sustain him as he develops those interests. Subtle and complex values can seldom if ever be understood and given the sanction of sympathy by the whole community; for companionship in his remoter developments of value the individual looks chiefly to sub-groups.

Moreover, a great part of the richness and variety of his life in a complex culture is created not by what he himself can do but by the delegated functioning carried out by specialists and their sub-groups. He cannot be a ballet dancer or an arctic explorer or an archaeologist, but as a member of the community which includes these people he has some part in their achievement. And in a culture as fluently communicative as ours he has opportunities—through biography, fiction, drama, the cinema and broadcasting—of going with imaginative insight some little way along the paths that other people have followed.

Life in a social group demands the capacity not only to enjoy social satisfactions, but also to tolerate some degree of frustration in social desire. Some of the inevitable frustration comes about through the necessity at times of opposing or seriously competing with people who are potentially friendly companions, the more competitive the culture the more extensive being the social frustration induced in this way. Relations with friendly colleagues who are also rivals consequently develop a high degree of complexity, or in less fully conscious people a high degree of incoherence and ambivalence; and a society like ours provides in compensation various forms of relaxation in which a simpler friendliness can be safely indulged. A more seriously disturbing deprivation of social needs occurs when the sense of having a function for the group is lost, as it was by the unemployed and as it still is by many people who retire from employment (and sometimes by mothers whose

children have grown up). The sense which besets some older people
of having no effective part in the community's life also troubles
others whose activities in middle life represent values too remote
from the dominant concerns of their community; their *malaise* may
appear overtly in a recognisable form of nostalgic distress or it may
by reaction-formation lead to the defiance and cultivated contempt
that mark the attitude of, for instance, some 'highbrows' to their
community. Their situation reveals the psychological inadequacy of
a sub-group that is too peripheral to the main concerns of its contemporary community, whatever its support from earlier tradition.
However, some of the most valuable work done in any generation,
especially work that leads to new developments in the group's
values, has to be done in the absence of social support, often in face
of opposition, and it demands, therefore, a capacity in the individual
to tolerate some frustration of social desire.

The social development of a human being involves the definition
of individuality as well as conformity to the broad features of
personality sanctioned by his particular culture. A group that tends
too one-sidedly to establish conformities among its members wastes
some part of its human resources; a more adequate group induces
in its members enough psychological security to tolerate their
differences from each other. An important difference between groups
(and between different periods in the history of the same group)
consists, therefore, in the degree to which they can elicit diversities
of ability, interest and sentiment among their individual members
without risking disruption or losing the power of effective corporate action when necessary. From one point of view, a society consists of people who are reciprocally sanctioning each other's interests
and standards. In consequence there are limits to the individual
deviations it will tolerate from its commoner (or its institutionalised)
modes of behaviour and varieties of outlook. Some it attempts to
eradicate or minimise by forms of social pressure, whether persuasion, ridicule or material punishment. Others it insulates as 'abnormal', so rendering them irrelevant to the social context (apart
from any material consequences their actions may have); it nullifies
any effect their example might have upon the values of other
members of the group. There are several, often confused and con-

flicting, criteria by which a group comes to judge a particular range of action and attitude as abnormal: but the social function of the judgement itself, that of minimising the social relevance of the behaviour, is fairly simple and consistent. A similar but less extreme mode of insulating some behaviour consists in permitting it as an oddity limited to a section of the group, a section which is identifiable by some other means besides the behaviour in question; thus some primitive peoples tolerate homosexuality, identifying the homosexuals by a clearly distinguished dress and way of life, while the laws of our society treat it as a 'bad' trait in a 'normal' person and have then to attempt suppression by punishment. An important part of any social order thus consists in finding ways of handling those who deviate from what is usual or otherwise established among members of the group.

Among the deviants are not only criminals, psychopaths and oddities but also those who, without being anti-social or mentally deranged, still have convictions and values very different from those current in their society and who, if they stick to the deviant values, are thereby brought into conflict with their group. Among them are people who carry their point successfully enough to be regarded by the group (either in their own day or later) as reformers or valuable innovators. The resistance commonly mobilised against an innovation serves the social functions of probing the weak points and excesses of the new point of view and of maintaining group stability and continuity with tradition; but the stability may easily become rigidity, and the reasonable scrutiny of the new idea may become a rationalisation of laziness, selfish vested interest, and the basic insecurity that makes all change frightening. Only when a large or influential part of a group possesses enough emotional security to relinquish the irrational processes that encourage clinging to the familiar is it possible for new possibilities to be judged on their merits.

Difficulties and wasteful tensions arising out of the work of innovators are part of a broader problem which every community faces, that of securing harmonious and mutually valuable relations between the 'common man' (to use a loose but convenient concept) and those who are outstanding. Defensive hostility towards high achievement of certain kinds (and towards even the admitted aim of working to higher standards in some directions) seems to arise from a fear that our own achievements are consequently being disparaged and our contentment questioned. In some circumstances this hostility results in serious obstruction and waste of talent. Jealousy of the able, pleasure in putting obstacles in the way of those who threaten to excel, gratification when the eminent come to grief, all these are ugly possibilities in the make-up of most of us about which we maintain a mutually considerate silence. It goes almost without saying that when needless tension exists between the average and the excellent both sides have probably helped to bring it about; where the former feel jealousy and chagrin the latter too commonly exhibit an equally insecure superciliousness and defiance.

More usually, of course, these acute strains are avoided, the relation being instead one of mutual wariness and armed neutrality. And in more fortunate and not infrequent circumstances there occurs the positive, eager alliance between the average and the outstanding—whether as subordinates and leader or audience and creative mind—that enhances the psychological security of each. At present, however, there is curiously little knowledge about the circumstances that make for satisfactory and less satisfactory relations between such people and it is not certain that we can even formulate the problems precisely and ask the right questions.

Yet few of us would doubt that hidden waste of human resources does occur as a result of unsatisfactory relations between the unusually able and the average. One aspect of the problem is seen in the attitude of older people towards abler young people who will eventually outdistance them. Another aspect appears in industry where the attitude of supervisors and executives towards the potential achievement of the abler people they control may notoriously be a source of friction. The same problem occurs no less clearly in the more complex, non-material aspects of culture. Here, too, the potential richness and subtlety of a society's cultural resources are partly lost through the lack of social techniques that will help the average to maintain their justifiable self-esteem and psychological security while recognising and welcoming the achievement of the outstanding and original. In a democracy, where the average among us tend eventually to get our way, the possibility of constantly developing our available fund of human resources demands techniques for helping those with special gifts to excel the rest of us.

REFERENCES

ADORNO, T. W., *et al.*, *The Authoritarian Personality*. New York: Harper, 1950.

ALBIG, W., *Public Opinion*. New York: McGraw Hill, 1939.

ALBINO, R. C. and LONG M., 'The effect of infant food-deprivation upon adult hoarding in the white rat'. *Brit. J. Psychol.* XLII, 1 and 2, 1951.

ALLEE, W. C., *The Social Life of Animals*. London: Heinemann, 1939.

ALLPORT, F. H., *Social Psychology*. Cambridge, Mass: Harvard University Press, 1924.

ALLPORT, G. W., *Personality*. London: Constable, 1938.

ANDERSON, H. H., 'Domination and integration in the behaviour of kindergarten children and teachers'. *Genetic Psychology Monographs*, Vol. 21, No. 3, 1939.

BARTLETT, F. C., *Psychology and Primitive Culture*. Cambridge University Press, 1923.

—— 'The social psychology of leadership'. *J. Nat. Inst. of Industrial Psychology*, III, 4, October, 1926.

BATESON, G. and MEAD, M., *Balinese Character*. New York: Academy of Sciences, 1942.

BEACH, Frank A., *Hormones and Behavior*. New York and London: Hoeber, 1948.

BENEDICT, Ruth, *Patterns of Culture*. London: Routledge, 1935.

—— *The Chrysanthemum and the Sword*. London: Secker and Warburg, 1947.

BION, W. R., *Experiences in Groups*. London: Tavistock, 1961.

BOWLBY, J., *Maternal Care and Mental Health*. Geneva: W.H.O., 1951.
—— 'The nature of the child's tie to his mother'. *Int. Jnl. Psycho-Analysis*, XXXIX, V, 1958.

BULLEY, Margaret, *Art for Everyman*. London: Batsford, 1952.

BURR, Anna Robeson, *Alice James: Her Brothers—Her Journal*. London: Macmillan, 1934.

BURROW, Trigant, *The Social Basis of Consciousness*. London: Kegan Paul, 1927.

CAMPBELL, W. J., 'The influence of home environment on the educational progress of selective secondary school children'. *Brit. J. Educ. Psychol.*, XXII, II, 1952.

CARTWRIGHT, D., and ZANDER, A. (eds.), *Group Dynamics*. 2nd ed. London: Tavistock, 1960.

CATTELL, R. B., 'New concepts for measuring leadership, in terms of group syntality', *Human Relations*, 4, 1951.

CHILD, L., POTTER, E. H., and LEVINE, E. M., 'Children's textbooks and personality development: an exploration in the social psychology of education'. *Psych. Monographs*, Vol. 60, 3, 1946.

CHOWN, S. M., 'Rigidity—a flexible concept', *Psychol. Bull.* 56, 3, 1959.

CULPIN, Millais and SMITH, May, 'The Nervous Temperament'. Industrial Health Research Board Report, No. 61. London: H. M. Stationery Office, 1930.

DARLING, F. Fraser, *Bird Flocks and the Breeding Cycle*. Cambridge University Press, 1938.

DAVIS, Norah, 'Some psychological effects on women workers of payment by the individual bonus method'. *Occupational Psychology*, XVIII, 1944.

DREVER, J., *Instinct in Man*, Cambridge University Press, 1917.

DU BOIS, Cora, *The People of Alor*. Minneapolis: University of Minnesota Press, 1944.

DURBIN, E. F. M. and BOWLBY, John, *Personal Aggressiveness and War*. London: Routledge, 1939.

DURET, T., *Manet and the French Impressionists*. London: Richards, 1909.

EDELSTON, H., 'Separation anxiety in young children: a study of hospital cases'. *Genetic Psychology Monographs*, Vol. 28, 1943.

FFRENCH, Yvonne, *Ouida: A Study in Ostentation*. London: Cobden-Sanderson, 1938.

FLEMING, Peter, *News from Tartary*. London: Cape, 1936.

FORTUNE, R. F., *Sorcerers of Dobu*. London: Routledge, 1932.

FOSS, B. M. (ed.), *Determinants of Infant Behaviour*. London: Methuen, 1961.

FOX, George, *The Journal*, revised by Norman Penney. London: Everyman's Library, 1924.

FOX, A. Lane, 'Primitive Warfare'. *Proceedings of the Royal United Service Institution*, II, 28th June, 1867.

FLUGEL, J. C., *Man, Morals and Society*. London: Duckworth, 1945.

FREUD, S., *Group Psychology and the Analysis of the Ego*. London: Hogarth Press, 1922.

FROMM, E., *The Fear of Freedom*. London: Kegan Paul, 1942.

FURFEY, P., 'A note on the relative development age scores of urban and rural boys'. *Child Development*, 6, 1935.

GINSBERG, M., *Studies in Sociology*. London: Methuen, 1932.
—— *Reason and Unreason in Society*. London: Longmans Green, 1947.

GLOVER, E., *War, Sadism and Pacifism*. London: Allen and Unwin, 1933.

GOLIGHTLY, C. L. and SCHEFFLER, I., 'Playing the dozens: a note'. *J. Abnorm. and Soc. Psych.*, 43, 1, 1948.

GORER, G., *The Americans: a study in national character*. London: Cresset Press, 1948.

—— and RICKMAN, J., *The People of Great Russia*. London: Cresset Press, 1949.

GRYGIER, T., 'The psychological problems of Soviet Russia'. *Brit. J. Psychol.*, XLII, 1 and 2, 1951.

GUEST, Lady Charlotte, *Extracts from her Journal*, 1833–1852, ed. by the Earl of Bessborough. London: Murray, 1950.

HARDING, D. W., 'A Note on Nostalgia' in *Determinations*, edited F. R. Leavis, London: Chatto and Windus, 1934.

—— *The Impulse to Dominate*. London: Allen and Unwin, 1941.

HARLOW, Harry F., and Harlow, Margaret K., 'The effect of rearing conditions on behavior'. *Bulletin of the Menninger Clinic*, 26 (5), 1962.

HARRIS, H., *The Group Approach to Leadership-Testing*. London: Routledge and Kegan Paul, 1949.

HAVIGHURST, R. and TABA, H., *Adolescent Character and Personality*. New York: Wiley, 1949.

HORNEY, K., *The Neurotic Personality of Our Time*. New York: Norton, 1937.

HUNT, J. McV., *et al.*, 'Studies of the effect of infantile experience on adult behaviour in rats. I. Effects of infantile feeding frustration'. *J. Comp. Psychol.*, XL, 1947.

HUNTER, W. S., 'Summary Comments on the Heredity-Environment Symposium'. *Psychological Review*, 54, 6, 1947.

ISAACS, S., *Social Development in Young Children*. London: Routledge, 1933.

ITARD, J. M. G., *The Wild Boy of Aveyron*, trans. G. and M. Humphrey. New York: The Century Co., 1932.

JAQUES, Elliott, *Measurement of Responsibility*. London: Tavistock, 1956.

JONES, Ernest, 'The concept of a normal mind'. *Int. J. of Psycho-Analysis*, XXIII, 1, 1942.

JUNG, C., *Modern Man in Search of a Soul*. London: Kegan Paul, 1933.

KATZ, David, *Animals and Men*. London: Longmans Green, 1937.

KNIGHT, Rex, *Intelligence and Intelligence Tests*. London: Methuen, 1933.

KÖHLER, W., *The Mentality of Apes*. London: Kegan Paul, 1925.

KRECH, D. and Crutchield, R. S., *Theory and Problems of Social Psychology*. New York: McGraw Hill, 1948.

KUO, Z. Y., 'The genesis of the cat's responses to the rat'. *J. Comp. Psychol.*, 11, 1, 1930.

LAPIERE, R. T. and Farnsworth, P. R., *Social Psychology*. New York: McGraw Hill, 1949.

LASSWELL, H. D., *World Politics and Personal Insecurity*. New York: McGraw Hill, 1935.

—— *Power and Personality*. London: Chapman and Hall, 1949.

LEIGHTON, Dorothea and KLUCKHOHN, Clyde, *Children of the People*. Cambridge, Mass.: Harvard University Press, 1948.

LEWIN, K., *Resolving Social Conflicts*. New York: Harper, 1948.

—— LIPPITT, R. and WHITE, R. K., 'Patterns of aggressive behaviour in experimentally created "social climates"'. *J. Soc. Psychol.*, 10, 1939.

LINTON, Ralph, *The Cultural Background of Personality*. London: Kegan Paul, 1947.

LORENZ, K., *King Solomon's Ring*. London: Methuen, 1952.

MCCANN, Willis, H., 'Nostalgia: a review of the literature'. *Psychol. Bulletin*, March, 1941.

MACCURDY, J. T., 'The Relation of Psychopathology to Social Psychology' in *The Study of Society*, edited F. C. Bartlett *et al.* London: Kegan Paul, 1939.

MCDOUGALL, W., *An Introduction to Social Psychology*. London: Methuen, 1908.

—— *The Energies of Men*. London: Methuen, 1932.

MACK, G., *Paul Cézanne*. New York: Knopf, 1935.

MCKELLAR, P., 'Provocation to anger and the development of attitudes of hostility'. *Brit. J. Psychol.*, XL, 3, 1950.

MACKENZIE-GRIEVE, Averil, *Last Years of the English Slave Trade*. London: Putnam, 1941.

MACKWOOD, John, 'The psychological treatment of offenders in prison'. *Brit. J. Psychol.*, XL, 1, 1949.

MAJUMDAR, D. N., *The Affairs of a Tribe*. Lucknow: Universal Publishers, 1950.

MASS OBSERVATION, *War Factory*. London: Gollancz, 1943.

MAYO, Elton, *The Human Problems of an Industrial Civilization*. New York, 1933.

MEAD, Margaret, *Coming of Age in Samoa*. London: Cape, 1929.

—— *Sex and Temperament in Three Primitive Societies*. London: Routledge, 1935.

—— (ed.), *Co-operation and Competition among Primitive Peoples*. New York: McGraw Hill, 1937.

METCALF, H. C. and Urwick, L. (eds.), *Dynamic Administration: the collected papers of Mary Parker Follet*. Bath: Management Publications Trust, 1941.

MIDDLEMORE, M. P., *The Nursing Couple*. London: H. Hamilton, 1941.

MILLER, Neal E. and DOLLARD, John, *Social Learning and Imitation.* London: Kegan Paul, 1945.

MOORE, B. V. and HARTMANN, G. W., *Readings in Industrial Psychology*. New York: Appleton, 1931.

MORENO, J. L., *Who Shall Survive?* Nervous and Mental Disease Monograph Series, No. 58. Washington: Nervous and Mental Disease Publishing Co., 1934.

MURPHY, G., MURPHY, L. B., and NEWCOMB, T. M., *Experimental Social Psychology*. New York and London: Harper, 1937.

ORLANSKY, Harold, 'Infant care and personality'. *Psychol. Bull.*, 46, 1, 1949.

ORWELL, George, *Homage to Catalonia*. London: Secker and Warburg, 1938.

PEAR, T. H., *The Psychology of Effective Speaking*. London: Kegan Paul, 1938.

—— *English Social Differences*. London: Allen and Unwin, 1955.

PIAGET, J., *The Moral Judgement of the Child*. London: Kegan Paul, 1932.

PRESSEY, S. L. and PRESSEY, L. C., 'Development of the interest-attitude tests'. *J. Appl. Psychol.*, 17, 1933.

READ, Herbert, *Poetry and Anarchism*. London: Freedom Press, 1935.

REAVELY, Constance and WINNINGTON, John, *Democracy and Industry*. London: Chatto and Windus, 1947.

RIESMAN, David, *The Lonely Crowd*. New Haven: Yale University Press, 1950.

ROETHLISBERGER, F. J. and DICKSON, W. J., *Management and the Worker*, Cambridge, Mass.: Harvard University Press, 1949.

SHERIF, M., *An Outline of Social Psychology*. New York: Harper, 1948.

SHERRINGTON, C. S., *The Integrative Action of the Nervous System*. New Haven: Yale University Press, 1906.

SLAVSON, S. R., *Analytic Group Psychotherapy*. New York: Columbia University Press, 1950.

SUTTIE, Ian D., *The Origins of Love and Hate*. London: Kegan Paul, 1935.

TAYLOR, C. W. (ed.), *Research Conference on the Identification of Creative Scientific Talent*. Salt Lake City: University of Utah Press, 1956.

TAYLOR, W. S., 'Basic personality in orthodox Hindu culture patterns'. *J. Abnorm. and Soc. Psychol.*, 43, 1, 1948.

TERHUNE, A. M., *The Life of Edward FitzGerald*. London: Oxford University Press, 1947.

THOMPSON, Laura, *Culture in Crisis: a study of the Hopi Indians*. New York: Harper, 1950.

THORPE, W. H., *Learning and Instinct in Animals*. 2nd ed. London: Methuen, 1963.

TROTTER, W., *Instincts of the Herd in Peace and War*. London: Fisher Unwin, 1916, and revised edition, 1919.

TRUAX, Rhoda, *Joseph Lister*. London: Harrap, 1947.

VEBLEN, T., *The Theory of the Leisure Class*. New York, Macmillan, 1899; reprinted London: Allen and Unwin, 1924.

WAITES, J. A., 'An inquiry into the attitude of adults towards property in a Lancashire urban area'. *Brit. J. Psychol.*, XXXVI, 1, 1945.

WARNER, W. L. and LUNT, P. S., *The Social Life of a Modern Community*. New Haven: Yale University Press, 1941.

WASHBURN, R. W., 'Reactions of children in a new social situation'. *J. Genetic Psychol.* XL, 1, 1932.

WEST, James, *Plainsville, U.S.A.* New York: Columbia University Press, 1945.

WESTERMARCK, Edward, *Ethical Relativity*. London: Kegan Paul, 1932.

WHITEHEAD, T. N., *Leadership in a Free Society*. Cambridge, Mass.: Harvard University Press, 1936.

WHITING, J. W. M. and CHILD, I. L., *Child Training and Personality*. New Haven: Yale University Press, 1953.

WILLOUGHBY, R. R., 'A scale of emotional maturity'. *J. Soc. Psychol.*, III, 1932.

WILSON, Mona, *The Life of William Blake*. London: Nonesuch Press, 1927.

WINNICOTT, D. W., 'Pediatrics and Psychiatry'. *Brit. J. Med. Psychol.*, 21, 229, 1948.

WOODWORTH, R. S., *Dynamic Psychology*. New York: Columbia University Press, 1918. Rewritten and enlarged as *Dynamics of Behavior*. London: Methuen, 1958.

WYATT, S., 'Incentives in Repetitive Work'. *Industrial Health Research Board Report*, No. 69. London: H. M. Stationery Office, 1934.

YOUNG, Kimball, *Handbook of Social Psychology*. London: Kegan Paul, 1946.

INDEX